AI and Big Data

ELGAR STUDIES IN LAW AND REGULATION

Series Editor: Roger Brownsword, *Professor of Law, King's College London, UK*

Regulation is a ubiquitous concept in today's world. The proliferation of new technologies necessitates continual re-appraisal of the rules that govern them, whilst globalization increases the complexity of interaction between governance systems on a national, regional and international level. As a field of study, regulation continues to grow and evolve, both in consideration of specific sectors, and at a conceptual level, as the rationale and motivation for regulation are scrutinized.

This new and exciting series is an important forum for original works of scholarship that explore regulation and its interaction with the law. It favours work that has a critical, innovative or analytical perspective and, whilst having a primary focus on legal writing, welcomes approaches that draw on other disciplines. The scope of the series encompasses a wide range of regulatory fields, from biotechnology and ICT to machine learning and AI, from security, food, and environment to health, leisure, and employment. At the same time the series plays host to broader discussions on the nature of risk, governance models, the role of democracy, regulatory theory and many others.

The primary mission of the series is to stimulate the development of original thinking across law and regulation and to foster the best theoretical and empirical scholarship in the field.

For a full list of Edward Elgar published titles, including the titles in this series, visit our website at www.e-elgar.com

AI and Big Data
Disruptive Regulation

Mark Findlay

Honorary Senior Fellow, British Institute of International and Comparative Law, United Kingdom – previously Director, Centre for AI and Data Governance, Singapore Management University, Singapore

Josephine Seah

PhD Candidate, University of Cambridge, United Kingdom; Affiliate, Centre for AI and Data Governance, Singapore Management University, Singapore

Willow Wong

Research Associate, Centre for AI and Data Governance, Singapore Management University, Singapore

ELGAR STUDIES IN LAW AND REGULATION

 Edward Elgar
PUBLISHING

Cheltenham, UK • Northampton, MA, USA

Published by
Edward Elgar Publishing Limited
The Lypiatts
15 Lansdown Road
Cheltenham
Glos GL50 2JA
UK

Edward Elgar Publishing, Inc.
William Pratt House
9 Dewey Court
Northampton
Massachusetts 01060
USA

A catalogue record for this book
is available from the British Library

Library of Congress Control Number: 2023942251

This book is available electronically in the **Elgar**online
Law subject collection
http://dx.doi.org/10.4337/9781802209525

ISBN 978 1 80220 951 8 (cased)
ISBN 978 1 80220 952 5 (eBook)

Printed and bound by CPI Group (UK) Ltd, Croydon, CR0 4YY

Contents

1. Disruptive regulation[1] [2]

DISRUPTION BEYOND *ECONOMY*

When *regulation* and *disruption* are usually linked in governance parlance, the intended meaning is to distil what are the most economically beneficial regulatory technologies and forms directed towards *disruptive innovation and market maximizing*.[3] The discussion that follows predictably focuses on how profit-enhancing regulatory objectives can be achieved with the softest touch possible. The reasoning for this approach is based on what now has been criticized as a problematic assumption – that disruptive innovation and the disruptive technologies it feeds are enlivening for the autonomy stakeholders and are uniquely profit generating for markets at large.[4] An aligned contestable assumption is that regulation dampens innovation, and that the stronger is the regulatory requirement, the weaker will be market advantage.[5]

Recently, the language of 'disruption' has been captured by those who wish to justify often unsustainable market practices under the guise of 'innovative' business models. In so doing disruption theory and its rich literature has been misrepresented.

[1]   This research is supported by the National Research Foundation, Singapore under its Emerging Areas Research Projects (EARP) Funding Initiative. Any opinions, findings and conclusions or recommendations expressed in this material are those of the author(s) and do not reflect the views of National Research Foundation, Singapore.
[2]   This chapter was written by Mark Findlay; Chapter 2 was written by Willow Wong; Chapter 3 was written by Mark Findlay; Chapter 4 was written by Josephine Seah; and Chapter 5 was written by Mark Findlay.
[3]   Nathan Cortez, 'Regulating Disruptive Innovation' (May 12, 2014) 29 *Berkeley Technology Law Journal*, SMU Dedman School of Law Legal Studies Research Paper No. 137, Available at SSRN:https://ssrn.com/abstract=2436065 or http://dx.doi.org/10.2139/ssrn.2436065 accessed 19 April 2023.
[4]   Justin Fox, The Disruption Myth (2014), *The Atlantic*, https://www.theatlantic.com/magazine/archive/2014/10/the-disruption-myth/379348/ accessed 19 April 2023.
[5]   Tung Hao-Lee, Does Financial Regulation Effect the Profit Efficiency and Risks of Banks: Evidence from China's Commercial Banks, (December 2013) 26 *The North American Journal of Economics and Finance* 705–724, DOI:10.1016/j.najef.2013.05.005 accessed 19 April 2023.

Unfortunately, disruption theory is in danger of becoming a victim of its own success. Despite broad dissemination, the theory's core concepts have been widely misunderstood and its basic tenets frequently misapplied. Furthermore, essential refinements in the theory over the past 20 years appear to have been overshadowed by the popularity of the initial formulation. As a result, the theory is sometimes criticized for shortcomings that have already been addressed.[6]

As the authors suggest, disruptive innovations originate in low end or new market footholds, and disruptive innovations do not catch on with mainstream customers/stakeholders until quality catches up to their standards. So, sustainability and originality are central to disruption as a market theory, and regulation will have a hand in ensuring both. Furthermore, we would argue that regulation can be disruptive if the sources of market disruption are turned towards sustainability and originality for the widest possible 'goods'.

The contemporary drivers of disruptive innovation are AI technologies and big data.[7] AI and big data, as such are seen as inherently *disruptive*, co-conspirators in destabilizing established market relationships and economic arrangements. Perhaps the only thing in the preceding sentences with which the book's position on disruptive regulation accords is that AI and big data have a potential for disruption. At this point we diverge into the argument that while AI and big data require vigorous regulatory oversight,[8] there is a distinct potential for AI and its use of data to assist in regulating the negative social consequences of disruptive innovation, particularly in the context of platform economies and their data reuse.[9] The purpose of this book is to investigate and establish AI and data usage as the solution and not the problem when responsible regulatory disruption is envisaged.

The case-studies in the body of this book explore how AI ethics and community (building trusted social bonds), digital self-determination (enabled in safe digital spaces), and disruptive innovation through cross-ecosystem communication (challenging the AI ethics/business profit paradigm) each provide

---

[6]   Christensen Clayton, Raynor Michael and McDonald Rory, 'What is Disruptive Innovation?', *Business Law Review* December 2015, https://hbr.org/2015/12/what-is-disruptive-innovation accessed 19 April 2023.

[7]   Moses Strydom and Sheryl Buckley, (eds), *AI and Big Data's Potentials for Disruptive Innovation (Advances in computational intelligence and robotics)*, 2019, ICI Global.

[8]   Understanding AI Governance.

[9]   Mark Findlay and Josephine Seah, 'Data Imperialism: Disrupting Secondary Data in Platform Economies Through Participatory Regulation' (May 29, 2020). SMU Centre for AI & Data Governance Research Paper No. 2020/06, Available at SSRN: https://ssrn.com/abstract=3613562 or http://dx.doi.org/10.2139/ssrn.3613562 accessed 19 April 2023.

testbeds where AI and data use collaborate in regulatory projects that disrupt conventional imaginings and operations of disruptive economies. Later in this chapter, some time is spent critiquing the exemplar of disruptive economies, platform commercial facilitation, to specifically reveal how AI-assisted information technologies can empower vulnerable market stakeholders and initiate new power dynamics in market arrangements. The purpose of this preparatory exercise is to suggest a regulatory model showing how AI and data usage can act in disruptive regulation. In our concluding reflections, this frame will be positioned within a novel understanding both of regulation and disruption in the AI age. A pressing need for the disruptive regulation incorporating AI and data usage as we suggest is heightened by arguments that AI is for social good and sustainable development without accompanying these assertions with a regulatory frame that shifts essential tech transformation power differentials. Our final speculation is that disruptive regulation can be an essential guarantee of inclusive and participatory socio-digital future making.

It is first necessary to settle on the essence of regulation out of which to craft disruption. In her definition of regulation, Julia Black posits the following features and outcomes:[10]

> ... the sustained and focused attempt to alter the behaviour of others according to defined standards or purposes with the intention of producing a broadly identified outcome or outcomes, which may involve mechanisms of standard-setting, information gathering and behaviour modification.

The theoretical underpinnings of this definition are:

– Pluralist and inclusive
– Facilitative to alter behaviour
– Evaluative in terms of effectiveness of techniques and methods
– Cognitive in terms of intention.

The current approaches to leading regulatory frames for governing AI and data usage (such as personal data protection legislation and ethics principles) do not exhibit these criteria beyond an intention for behavioural change toward trusted technology. Ethical AI has been criticized for being neither inclusive nor pluralist (see Chap 2) and many of the more command and control rights protection strategies are rarely evaluated in terms such as data subject satisfaction. It is the failure of prevailing regulatory modes to explore the power

---

[10]   Julia Black, 'Constitutionalizing Self-regulation' (1996) *Modern Law Review*, 59(1) 24–55.

differentials that underlie tech transformation and mass data sharing that this text wishes to disrupt and reverse.

Turning the regulatory purpose away from the maximizing of market profit via disruptive economies and back to the protection and advancement of vulnerable stakeholders and their interests, then it makes sense that any regulatory technique advancing such a redirected objective will disrupt the current 'light touch' market approach with its roots firmly grounded in exclusive wealth creation.[11]

Black's definition requires an intentional and conscious intervention for changing the direction of otherwise unregulated (or under-regulated) activity and its motivations in an empirically measurable manner. This is a far cry from the presently preferred regulatory frame for AI and its data use, being voluntary ethical compliance. As a voluntary self-regulation regime, it carries all the criticisms of soft and self-interested regulatory intervention.[12] At the same time it is commended as being consistent with the economic purposing of disruptive innovation.[13]

Returning to Black's definition, regulation is intended for behavioural change. But whose behaviour is to be altered and how? In the 'soft regulation maximises disruptive innovation'[14] thinking regulation should do as little to alter the market trajectory of tech and data use as possible. Such a scenario redirects behavioural change away from information gathering purposes that deepen the regulator's knowledge of the challenge, and towards the broadest standard-setting purposes never intended to question or dampen profitability. Behavioural change is to some extent inverted. Regulation should be dominated by innovation so that the behaviour and objectives of regulation must change to fit market imperatives and not vice versa.

---

[11]   Harry Armstrong, Chris Gorst and Jen Rae, 'Renewing Regulation: Anticipatory Regulation in an Age of Disruption', (2019) *Nesta*London.

[12]   Josephine Seah and Mark Findlay, 'Communicating Ethics across the AI Ecosystem' (July 29, 2021). SMU Centre for AI & Data Governance Research Paper No. 07/2021, Available at SSRN: https://ssrn.com/abstract=3895522 or http://dx.doi.org/10.2139/ssrn.389552 accessed 19 April 2023.

[13]   Yoshua Bengio, 'Prioritising Ethical Principles in the Governance of Disruptive Technologies', 2021, European Parliament Research Service, https://epthinktank.eu/2021/05/18/prioritising-ethical-principles-in-the-governance-of-disruptive-technologies/ accessed 19 April 2023.

[14]   A market-oriented determination of disruptive innovation focuses on small enterprises with less resources is able to successfully challenge incumbent businesses. We take this view to a deeper level, by asking what externalities are necessary for this power dispersal to occur. One such is the valuing of ideas in the achievement of market positioning. Ideas and knowledge as values of innovation disrupt a reductionist neo-liberal market motivation.

The soft regulatory preferences for disruptive innovation and econo-mies might be further impeached for relying on two suspect presumptions. In free market thinking it is believed that market dynamics will regulate adverse market behaviour. This market natural selection can only be argued where markets are not themselves constrained by externalities which impede 'freedom'. Connected is the second presumption that disruptive economies thrive in competitive environments. One of the claims by disruptors that their incursions benefit the market by shaking up established, uncompetitive market players could be challenged against harmful market relationships (particularly in employment settings) advanced by disruptors and disadvantaging other incumbents who are required to respect established market conventions. In their paper 'Unfair Disruption' Lemley and McKenna observe this about anti-competitive disruptive economies:

> ...Incumbents frequently want to stop, or at least limit the use of, new technologies. And they often reach for intellectual property (IP), unfair competition, or related legal doctrines as tools to do so. The justification for stopping or limiting the use of new technologies follows a familiar pattern: incumbents claim that the new entrants undermine fundamental values of the existing industry and make the world worse off. If the new technology is allowed to proliferate, incumbents often argue, no one will ever make music (or movies, or any other creative or inventive output) again... Many IP, unfair competition, and related cases, then, are really about whether com-petition from new players can force incumbents to change their business models, generally to the advantage of particular players and the detriment of others.[15]

This selective benefit/detriment duality has been shown to have greater adverse influence on vulnerable stakeholders such as workers and customers.[16] If the loss of competition is as a consequence of unfair market behaviour (such as that exemplified in the example later in this chapter) then the disruption will disadvantage incumbents AND the market. In addition, notable market disrupters have consolidated with incumbents to exclude competition or have preyed on smaller competitors to oligopolise market share.[17]

The case for *disruptive regulation*, in the theoretical analysis that com-prises this chapter and in the contextual settings of the chapters to follow, is

---

[15] Mark Lemely and Mark McKenna, 'Unfair Disruption', (2020) *Boston University Law Review* 100: 100–163 at 104.

[16] Mabel Choo Zi Ling and Mark Findlay, 'Platform Workers, Data Dominion and Challenges to Work-life Quality' (May 3, 2021). SMU Centre for AI & Data Governance Research Paper No. 04/2021, Available at SSRN: https://ssrn.com/abstract=3839873 or http://dx.doi.org/10.2139/ssrn.3839873 accessed 19 April 2023.

[17] Bernoit Chevalier-Roignant, Christoph Flath, and Lenos Trigeorgis, 'Disruptive Innovation, Market Entry and Production Flexibility in Heterogeneous Oligopoly', (2019) 28(7) *Production and Operations Management* 1641–1657.

intended to regain the potency of regulation when AI and big data are part of disruptive innovation and their technologies. The argument in its simplest form anticipates that rather than only being the regulatory subject (or indeed the regulatory challenge), AI and the data it employs can be integrated into the behavioural change agenda to achieve regulatory outcomes where technology and data use are beyond standards that are only set within the market imperatives of disruptive economies. AI, particularly where it provides information pathways to assist vulnerable stakeholders to more meaningfully participate in the regulatory project, offers the focus and sustainability to deflect or redirect the negative social consequences of disruptive innovation/economies.[18]

This introduction will lay the groundwork for understanding and practically applying disruptive regulation as we see it. In the next chapters the themes of community/ethics/trust, digital self-determination and responsible innovation through communication are concepts and contexts in which the dynamics and determinants of disruptive regulation are progressed. Commencing with the discussion of AI in community, embedded by social bonds of mutual trust, community-centric ethics as a regulatory discourse is materialized in the sustainable relationships between AI and humans. Digital self-determination re-invigorates data subjects in the management of their personal data and that of their communities by using AI to create and sustain safe digital spaces. Disruptive innovation through communication as our final case-study expounds away from the paradigm offered at the commencement of this section, portraying innovation pipelines as communication pathways in which principled design moves to responsible deployment, adhering to informed, ethical and inclusive organizational engagement.

Before venturing into the modelling and application of disruptive regulation it is useful to reflect on more conventional considerations of AI governance, and in particular, the way regulating AI and big data depends for its sustainability on pre-existing engagement with community recipients and data subjects. Such a re-ordering of regulatory obligation is the first step in disruptive regulation.

REGULATION AND AI INNOVATION – NEW DIRECTIONS

In general, and beyond disruptive innovation, the common association between AI, big data, and regulation centres on the appropriate (and deliverable) approaches to governing risk posed by technology and data use. Concerns

---

[18]   These negative social consequences will be materialized in the contexts and regulatory challenges discussed in the chapters to follow.

about the safety, robustness and risk aversion of the technology sees the regulatory gaze directed back into the lab and the factory and searches for standardization, conformity assessment, and legal controls as constituting regulatory measurement. Important as these may be for the initiation of community trust in AI and data use, they are not sufficient to maintain trusted bonds between humans and machines that would comprise important regulatory objectives. If behaviour is to change regarding the human/machine interface the intention needs to be more than risk management but disruptive cocreation.

The prevailing neoliberal notion of disruption is the rejection of conventional (and trusted over time) market relationships. In such settings AI and data use again are viewed as internal to the market and preconceived in regulatory objectives that favour exclusionist wealth creation.[19] They become the tools and language of individualist wealth maximising and thereby 'disrupt' fundamental social bonds such as worker welfare and employer obligation (on which conventional propensities for productivity have been based). This elemental disruption not only changes business models but can fracture work-life experience and endanger long-term market viability and social sustainability.

This book is interested in neither. It is intended here to reposition both regulation and disruption on two levels. Areas such as trust, ethics, principled design, responsible innovation, trustworthy technology, and data protection through various models currently are top-down compliance/risk minimization endeavours.[20] Alternatively, disruptive regulation utilises AI/big data (as objects and operatives) by disrupting both the trajectory of self-interested regulation and its reliance on abstracted behavioural change mechanisms never intended for social good. Instead, disruptive regulation proposes a communitarian, ecosystem focus for the attribution and distribution of regulatory responsibility so that it empowers stakeholders (such as data-subjects) who up until now if recognized at all are seen in vague paternalist terms. Each of the case-study chapters takes up the ecosystem approach both to the regulatory challenges and their solution, returning AI and data usage back to its presently disempowered subjects and communities. In addition, they examine decision sites (whether in the form of trust relationships, individualized and communal data management, or organizational cross-fertilized responsible innovation) to appreciate how AI/human interaction can evolve with mutual fairness and respect at its heart.

---

[19] Mark Findlay, *Globalisation, Populism, Pandemics and the Law: The Agony and the Ecstasy,* (Cheltenham: Edward Elgar, 2021).

[20] Josephine Seah and Mark Findlay, 'Communicating Ethics across the AI Ecosystem' (July 29, 2021). SMU Centre for AI & Data Governance Research Paper No. 07/2021, Available at SSRN: https://ssrn.com/abstract=3895522 or http://dx.doi .org/10.2139/ssrn.3895522 accessed 19 April 2023.

The second, and more disruptive level is that AI/big data become part of the regulatory solution and not just the regulatory challenge. Communitarian location and ecosystem engagement are developed to specifically reveal how this can be so. For instance, if regulation is pitted against market bias, wishing to change the behaviour of managers away from operational prejudice and towards equitable employment practices, AI can flag bias blind-spots and the algorithms transacting data can flag when conclusions from analysis step outside ethical boundaries. The regulatory model developed in the second half of this chapter expands the essential commitments to inclusion, representation and empowerment through AI information dispersal and data emancipation to vulnerable stakeholders.

In the critical literature, considerations about regulation and governance of AI from the aspirational cloud-space of AI ethics is progressing into a more nuanced discussion of ethics as part of a more complex and action-oriented regulatory tapestry.[21] The old language of personal data protection, rights to privacy and principled design is being overtaken by the recognition that trust in AI, dignity in data use, and responsibility in innovation should underpin more multi-faceted understandings of regulation and governance.[22] Particularly with the use and management of mass data, contentions concerning ownership and the protection of property rights are being assailed by the realization that data is not alienable, and that access and trade benefits can outweigh exclusive possession and licensed applications.[23]

REGULATION FUNDAMENTALS – BUILDING THE DISRUPTIVE FRAME

In approaching any regulatory enterprise there are four fundamental and pre-determining questions influencing the ultimate regulatory choice and direction:

---

[21] Mark Findlay, 'Ethics, Rule of Law and Pandemic Responses' (July 27, 2020). SMU Centre for AI & Data Governance Research Paper No. 2020/07, Available at SSRN: https://ssrn.com/abstract=3661180 or http://dx.doi.org/10.2139/ssrn.3661180 accessed 19 April 2023.

[22] Mark Findlay and Josephine Seah, 'An Ecosystem Approach to Ethical AI and Data Use: Experimental reflections' (May 12, 2020). SMU Centre for AI & Data Governance Research Paper No. 2020/03, Available at SSRN: https://ssrn.com/abstract =3597912 or http://dx.doi.org/10.2139/ssrn.3597912 accessed 19 April 2023.

[23] Nydia Remolina and Mark Findlay, 'The Paths to Digital Self-Determination – A Foundational Theoretical Framework' (April 22, 2021). SMU Centre for AI & Data Governance Research Paper No. 03/2021, Available at SSRN: https://ssrn.com/abstract =3831726 or http://dx.doi.org/10.2139/ssrn.3831726 accessed 19 April 2023.

Why – the simple answer is that because as many modern regulatory projects confront practices of technology that use, store, or disseminate personal data which are insufficiently managed by data subjects, then these should not proceed without responsible data governance.[24] But the matter is not so simple. Counter-narratives mentioned already which advance market over social applications for technology and data use too often necessitate for regulators the requirement to balance objective challenges to privacy and data integrity against strongly articulated economic well-being assumptions achieved through data reuse. Regulatory balancing opens up another line of debate which characterizes recent public resistance to the containment of liberties in movement and association inherent in COVID control measures.[25] Are the control justifications for employing personal data and restricting liberties valid, or indeed excessive, and if so who should be responsible for moderating these?[26] Thus, the *why regulate* question becomes difficult to isolate from the consent, compliance, good-will or even reluctant acquiescence of the data subject, as well as the competing interests that weigh on valuing and preferring personal data integrity over wealth creation and powerful forces of commercial

---

[24]   Muller Trix, 'Health Apps, Their Privacy Policies and the GDPR' (2019) 10(1) *European Journal of Law and Technology*; Bobby Fung, In this time of the coronavirus, does personal data privacy get thrown out the window?, *Withers World Wide* (20 March 2020) https://www.withersworldwide.com/en-gb/insight/in-this-time-of-covid -19-does-personal-data-privacy-get-thrown-out-the-window accessed 19 May 2020; European Patients Forum, The new EU Regulation on the protection of personal data: what does it mean for patients? (2018), https://www.eu-patient.eu/globalassets/policy/ data-protection/data-protection-guide-for-patients-organisations.pdf accessed 19 April 2023.

[25]   'Human Rights Dimensions of COVID-19 Response', *Human Rights Watch* (19 March 2020), https://www.hrw.org/news/2020/03/19/human-rights-dimensions-covid -19-response accessed 6 April 2020; European Union Agency for Fundamental Rights, *Coronavirus Pandemic in the EU - Fundamental Rights Implications,* Bulletin #1 (20 March 2020) https://fra.europa.eu/sites/default/files/fra_uploads/fra-2020-coronavirus -pandemic-eu-bulletin_en.pdf accessed 18 May 2020; Becky Beaupre Gillespie, 'In the fight against COVID-19, how much freedom are you willing to give up?' *University of Chicago News* (13 April 2020) https://news.uchicago.edu/story/fight-against-covid-19 -how-much-freedom-are-you-willing-give accessed 18 May 2020.

[26]   Suzanne Nossel, Don't Let Leaders Use the Coronavirus as an Excuse to Violate Civil Liberties, Foreign Policy (30 April 2020) https://foreignpolicy.com/2020/04/ 13/governments-coronavirus-pandemic-civil-liberties/ accessed 19 May 2020; Martin Bull, *Beating Covid-19: The problem with national lockdowns*, The London School of Political Science, EUROPP / European Politics and Policy Blog (26 March 2020) https://blogs.lse.ac.uk/europpblog/2020/03/26/beating-covid-19-the-problem-with -national-lockdowns/ (accessed 18 May 2020).

self-interest.[27] We would say that these antipathies can be recognized but the current obsession with market prioritizing needs rewriting against genuine behavioural change for social good outcomes.

When – again the simple answer is that the regulatory timetable should be inextricably determined by the urgency for behavioural change arising from the risks of inaction or mal-adaptation. Change must as well be driven by the provision of public vision and the maintenance of sustainable markets particularly for personal data. But whether it is because of doubts about the harm/value coefficients of disruptive innovation, regulatory modelling, or the quantification of tolerable risk to data integrity, even regulatory agendas are contested by competing agendas for the status quo or for change – personal profit against public good. These objectives need not be antipathetic when it comes to the responsible application of tech and data to disruptive regulation. In avoiding inconsequential deliberations over when it is prudent or profitable enough to be concerned enough about personal data use, regulators can suggest it is more productive to get protections in place as the market rolls out further disruptive innovation. The regulatory strategy (as detailed later in this chapter), to avoid market capture, needs to advocate that there is no disruptive innovation too valuable whatever the social harms it poses, or no personal data too insignificant to obviate the need for regulatory oversight.

Where – again answered simply, wherever the personal data produced through disruptive innovation is stored, accessed, used and in particular (as discussed later) reused, particularly if this behaviour disadvantages otherwise vulnerable stakeholders. Yet in the spirit that data has value for those on whose behalf we regulate, regulatory activity, its location and reach will depend on how much the regulatory recipient wants something to be done and done now. These concerns are often not a straightforward process of balancing legitimate preferences when certain stakeholders have little or no knowledge about the nature and extent of data use. Recourse to a vague language of universal rights does not replace more informed aspirations of the need and options (and impediments for change). And in some circumstances data subjects are complicit in errant data use. Take for instance in the case of social media data, there seems little doubt that the value of personal privacy is militated by access to private space, and familiarity with rights protections, along with the predatory pre-conditions for using some platforms.[28] One of the reasons that inclusive

[27] Mark Findlay, *Law's Regulatory Relevance: Property, Power and Market Economies* (Cheltenham: Edward Elgar, 2019).

[28] Charles Raab and Benjamin Goold, *Protecting information privacy,* Equality and Human Rights Commission Research report 69 (2011) https://www .equalityhumanrights.com/sites/default/files/research-report-69-protecting-information -privacy.pdf accessed 19 April 2023. The rights discourse is present even in Asian

self-regulation is later advanced in this chapter, resides in the appreciation that information deficits often found the disinterest of data subjects about significant threats to personal data integrity.

What – regulatory techniques range across a continuum of command and control to the least intrusive compliance formats.[29] Where any regulatory initiative sits on that continuum will depend on the urgency for a regulatory outcome, cooperation with or resistance against regulatory intent, and the extent to which regulatory needs can be quarterized from other unconnected or competing regulatory demands. This latter consideration is prominent when competing pressures exert to protect data or otherwise to enable access for different purposes and priorities. It should be conceded that the prevailing regulatory approach in governing AI and data use has been top-down, voluntary self-regulatory compliance. As our later critique of AI ethics reveals, the reasons behind supporting this approach may have as much to do with protecting against external regulatory intervention as they do with recognizing moral imperatives in regulatory discourse.

Another important determinant when choosing a preferred regulatory technology[30] is the extent to which regulatory recipients identify the need for behavioural change outcomes.[31] The process of identifying need will no doubt

---

countries that do not always include a 'right to privacy' in their legal and constitutional regimes. Asian courts with the most developed privacy jurisprudence frequently use similar language to protect privacy. Courts have found privacy to be an implied right based on protections of dignity and autonomy interests, such as personality development and informational self-determination. In defining valid restrictions on the constitutional right of privacy, the courts have adopted strikingly similar legal tests. Graham Greenleaf, 'The Right to Privacy in Asian Constitutions', *in The Oxford Handbook of Constitutional Law in Asia, Forthcoming* (2020) https://papers.ssrn.com/sol3/papers .cfm?abstract_id=3548497 accessed 19 April 2023.

[29] Mark Findlay, 'Corporate Sociability: Analysing Motivations for Collaborative Regulation', Research Collection Singapore Management University School Of Law 5-2014 (2014), (2014) 46(4) *Administration and Society* 339–370 https://ink.library .smu.edu.sg/cgi/viewcontent.cgi?article=4001&context=sol_research accessed 19 April 2023.

[30] In talking of optional regulatory 'technologies' this refers to the style of regulation (both in substance and application), not to be confused with any technology against which regulation might be directed.

[31] Bernard Marr, 'COVID-19 Is Changing Our World – And Our Attitude To Technology And Privacy –Why Could That Be Dangerous?', *Forbes* (23 March 2020) https://www.forbes.com/sites/bernardmarr/2020/03/23/covid-19-is-changing -our-world--as-well-as-our-attitude-to-technology-and-privacy-why-could-that-be-a -problem/#45c68cdd6dc1 accessed 18 May 2020; Salma Khalik, 'Coronavirus: Expect a New Normal Even if Current Circuit Breaker Measures are Eased', *The Straits Times Singapore* (7 May 2020) https://www.straitstimes.com/singapore/expect-a-new -normal-even-if-current-measures-are-eased accessed 18 May 2020; Marco Albani,

lead to contestation over advancing interests. This is why there needs to be a clear commitment to disrupting the soft underbelly of current regulatory policy if behavioural change is to benefit the presently forgotten.

Who – a common failing of regulatory overviews is to stipulate responsibility without specific attribution. Of course, in some instances, the nature of the regulatory technology will indicate its authority and trajectory. Command and control approaches require state sponsorship. Self-regulation invites more diverse stakeholder participation. However, there is a need to identify conundrums that attach to attribution and distribution of responsibility:

- Regulatory attribution is often most efficient when it is a collective endeavour. Public and private sector providers and administrators of innovation technology transmit common due diligence and best practice obligations because of the benefits they gain in any market sense. Civil society, when empowered through information access and understanding, should carry reporting and community oversight functions, provided they are given sufficient recognition, capacity and presence to enable potent participation in the regulatory exercise. Social and conventional media represent an important public education function and a facility for accountable debate provided reporting does not degenerate into misinformation or propaganda for any particular dogma.[32] The dark side of all these potential regulatory participants is how they are easily captured by the contentious self-interests

---

'There is no Returning to Normal after COVID-19. But there is a Path Forward', *World Economic Forum* (15 April 2020) https://www.weforum.org/agenda/2020/04/covid -19-three-horizons-framework/ accessed 27 April 2020; Shruti Bhargava, Courtney Buzzell, Christina Sexauer, Tamara Charm, Resil Das, Cayley Heller, Michelle Fradin, Grimmelt, Janine Mandel, Kelsey Robinson, Abhay Jain, Sebastian Pflumm, Anvay Tewari and Christa Seid, 'Consumer Sentiment Evolves as the Next "normal" Approaches', McKinsey & Company (12 May 2020) https://www.mckinsey.com/ business-functions/marketing-and-sales/our-insights/a-global-view-of-how-consumer -behavior-is-changing-amid-covid-19 accessed 18 May 2020; Cass R Sunstein, 'The Meaning of Masks', Forthcoming *Journal of Behavioral Economics for Policy* (2020) https://ssrn.com/abstract=3571428 accessed 19 April 2023.
[32]   Gordon Pennycook, Jonathon McPhetres, Yunhao Zhang and David G Rand, 'Fighting COVID-19 Misinformation on Social Media: Experimental Evidence for a Scalable Accuracy Nudge Intervention', *MIT Initiative on the Digital Economy* Working Paper (2020) http://ide.mit.edu/sites/default/files/publications/Covid-19 %20fake%20news%20ms_psyarxiv.pdf accessed 19 April 2023; R Jayaseelan, D Brindha, Kades Waran, *Social Media Reigned by Information or Misinformation About COVID-19: A Phenomenological Study,* Social Sciences & Humanities Open D-20-00130 (2020), https://papers.ssrn.com/sol3/papers.cfm?abstract_id=3596058 accessed 19 April 2023.

of powerful regulatory subjects (such as the platform owners examined in the model to follow).

- Where personal data is being shared by different private communication platforms and between public and private providers private law through service contracts is likely to create regulatory obligations on these entities for the benefit of their customers. As is discussed with data reuse later in this section and focused on specifically when we talk of digital self-determination, too often it is the clandestine context of such reuse and the consequent ignorance of the data subject that makes AI-assisted information looping so important as a regulatory disruptor. An example of breaching private law contract secrecy that may inhibit regulatory openness is by administrations requiring public contract arrangements with the private sector for the provision of public services.

- Public law in the form of data protection instruments may vest authority in independent agencies to perform regulatory functions. Independent regulation institutions and processes are particularly prominent when the purpose is to generate trust in the data management regime. Absent in most of these institutional regulatory frames is sufficient concern to engage with data subjects and their communities to inform them of the data challenges posed by disruptive innovation, and the possibilities of introducing into such innovation regulatory disruptors that 'red-light' where potential personal data abuse can occur, particularly in terms of biased representations and conclusions.

- Ultimately, and in a simple configuration when addressing regulatory attribution, the model detailed below progresses with this rule of thumb; *depending on who it is that advocates and promotes and administers disruptive economy/innovation technologies automatically producing personal data that could be misused, or to the harm of the data subject, then the responsibility to build in regulatory strategies to avoid harm and misuse rests initially with them.* The first step in discharging this responsibility is to ensure that AI technologies using personal data possess the capacity to inform data subjects and activate this routinely. Information deficits are at the heart of power asymmetries in data access flows and require addressing through the information tech that produces such deficits in the first place.

Acknowledging these peremptory questions/concerns, the regulatory model that follows rests on several prevailing regulatory maxims, when it comes to personal data integrity, and the use of AI and big data for disruptive innovation. In most jurisdictional strategies, regional conventions and international instruments, there is recognition of the necessity to protect personal data, both in the interests of the data subject and for the integrity of the data itself.[33] However, this recognition is being tempered by a growing concern that too much protection will unnecessarily impede access for innovation. While the limitations on personal data protection, and privacy regulation more generally are widely understood,[34] and there is often contention surrounding what is a challenge to personal data and privacy,[35] constitutional rights of privacy and administrative/legislative activity for the protection of personal data are a regulatory grounding that is far from universal across the globe. Additionally, the technologies employed in the data accumulation for disruptive innovation use big data or rely on internet-based communication pathways and as such should have the benefit of more over-arching regulatory regimes to reward responsible access that considers personal integrity. One reason why even larger regulatory paradigms for protecting mass data use and sharing have been patchy at best is that expansive AI information management dimensions place regulatory options inevitably alongside corporate, national, and international self-regulatory regimes which employ (or at least portend to employ) ethical principles governing the use of AI and big data. Critically leveraging these pre-existing supports, disruptive regulation within an AI/data governance tapestry provides a new perspective on responsibility for decisions, behaviours and relationships which previously were considered in protective/profit, or predatory/problematic dualities.

There is a groundswell of public opinion questioning the data safety of platform technologies in particular (detailed later in this chapter) and asking for guarantees that the use of personal data will be limited to the exigencies of the data subjects' interests ahead of the platform's proprietary claims.[36] Necessarily, the choice of preferred regulatory mode will be influenced by private contracts which consumers (and app users) negotiate with mobile com-

---

[33]   Graham Greenleaf, 'Global Data Privacy Laws 2019: 132 National Laws & Many Bills' (2019) 157 Privacy Laws & Business International Report 14–18 https:// papers.ssrn.com/sol3/papers.cfm?abstract_id=3381593 accessed 19 April 2023; Paul M Schwartz and Karl-Nikolaus Peifer, 'Transatlantic Data Privacy' (2017) 106 *Georgetown Law Journal* 115 https://papers.ssrn.com/sol3/papers.cfm?abstract_id= 3066971 accessed 19 April 2023.

[34]   Greenleaf, ibid.; Schwartz and Peifer, ibid.

[35]   Sebastian F Winter and Stefan F Winter, 'Human Dignity as Leading Principle in Public Health Ethics: A Multi-Case Analysis of 21st Century German Health Policy Decisions' (2018) 7(3) *International Journal of Health Policy Management* 210–224 http://www.ijhpm.com/article_3374.html accessed 19 April 2023.

[36]   See Mabel Choo, Zi Ling and Mark Findlay, 'Platform Workers, Data Dominion and Challenges to Work-life Quality' (May 3, 2021). SMU Centre for AI & Data Governance Research Paper No. 04/2021, Available at SSRN: https://ssrn.com/abstract =3839873 or http://dx.doi.org/10.2139/ssrn.3839873 accessed 19 April 2023.

munication providers, and the privacy policies of social media platforms and private and public data collectors and processors that may run contrary to any of the data-sharing practices that benefit disruptive innovation. Recognizing any regulatory counter-narrative which private law arrangements may portend, it is important for a disruptive regulatory strategy to be prepared to invade the boundaries of private law entitlements through challenging property rights claims and promoting associated grassroots resistance to such claims.[37]

Regulatory priorities may vary depending on their political, economic, and social context. For instance, in places where cultures of habitation are more communal, personal 'space' is limited, social hierarchies are intrusive, economic conditions exploitative, or styles of governance authoritarian, then privacy claims may be less well enunciated and understood, or respected and actionable. Even so, there are fundamental and universal characteristics which attend on human dignity, humane society and inclusive governance that should be a core aspirational focus of personal data regulation. And if the use of trans-jurisdictional technologies that transact privacy is not qualified by situational variations like different cultural locations to the detriment of data subject interests, all the more that technology should be inveigled into the common disruptive regulation project aiming at behavioural change for public benefit.

It is not intended here to re-iterate the reservations associated with a dominant ethics-principled approach to the governance of AI and big data which is detailed in our research publication on the matter and examined in the chapters to follow.[38] Power differentials internal to the AI ecosystem, market and client pressures and profitability demands militate against ethics as a sole effective regulator of AI and big data. In addition, the generality of the principles espoused in most ethical guidelines make them difficult to apply on all context-specific, or situationally relative bases. Therefore, regarding the regulatory approaches outlined to come, ethical aspirations form a strong normative morality which should pervade regulation's particular purposes and directions and test key decisions in the ecosystem. However, as with all voluntary compliance modes ethics is goodwill dependent and many disruptive economies consciously reject pre-existing market responsibilities and obligations.

The importance of human/individual dignity, to underpin the beneficial priorities of social good as a primary motivation for disruptive regulation necessitates an actionable frame. In what follows the significance of fairness, an anti-harm consciousness, and above all transparency and accountability will

---

[37] Elaborated on and examples provided in Findlay (2019), chap. 3.
[38] Mark Findlay and Josephine Seah, 'An Ecosystem Approach to Ethical AI and Data Use', SMU Centre for AI & Data Governance Research Paper No. 2020/03 (2020) https://papers.ssrn.com/sol3/papers.cfm?abstract_id=3597912 accessed 19 April 2023.

recur. But so will the demand to translate principle into regulatory practice which specifically confronts and counteracts market arrangements inconsistent with these intentions.

The argument for disruptive regulation is complex but will be made out as the case-studies evolve. To provide a foundation for how disruptive regulation can be applied in and through trust relationships, safe digital spaces, and community-responsible innovation it is now essential to give some wider consideration to the form and purpose of any proposed disruptive regulatory strategy, which will be attempted via the following snapshot of platform economies as disruptive innovation in the later parts of this chapter.

At a more general level, there are several different structural approaches to disruptive regulation that present themselves. These approaches are not unique to our concept of disruptive regulation, in fact they could apply to the activation of any regulatory strategy. However, particularly in the case of disruptive regulation, a unique interpretation of regulatory challenges from the perspective of vulnerable stakeholders in the market and their protection above the 'non-community' motivated profitability of disruptive innovation gives special meaning to these imperatives:

–   Highlight an essential regulatory obligation which binds together all the possible challenges posed by disruptive innovation and consequent data use – This *central theme approach* runs the risk of down-playing or bypassing other important themes. Yet, with disruptive regulation the core concern is oppositional to the current fascination of disruptive innovation – higher market positioning for self-interested wealth creation.
–   Follow a more conventional pattern and link regulatory techniques to individual data-use challenges – The difficulty with this approach is that it tends to become repetitive and is too causally dependent. Even so, by selecting data use in platform economies as something requiring regulatory behavioural change there is the potential to draw parallels with other contexts and agendas of 'public good'.
–   Group the challenges to personal data integrity under ethical principles and good governance best practice, and from there consolidate regulatory responses. This approach seems formalist and may tend to predetermine regulatory selection. Again, it has the benefit of interrogating the actuality of a prominent normative frame behind presently popular regulatory approaches.
–   Reverse the 'principled' approach by setting out a menu of likely and appropriate regulatory technologies and then group data challenges under these options. This method has the advantage of identifying the regulatory sponsors (state/industry/civil society) more directly and attributing and distributing particularist responsibilities for behavioural change. Once this

is done, the principled frame can be reintroduced to measure the relative legitimacy of regulatory technologies and the appropriateness of their selection.

To make the choice and extrapolate the potentials of a disruptive regulatory strategy more focussed, accessible, and relevant to an audience with different views on regulatory needs and outcomes thereby, the strategy will be framed around three encompassing humanitarian aspirations for the regulatory exercise.

1. *Lessen and avoid discrimination* – there are market contexts for these disruptive innovation technologies such as service-delivery platforms, wherein certain stakeholder understandings of coverage and data-use consequences, of discriminatory access and usage against vulnerable groups such as workers and customers, require that wider consciousness building for the lessening of discrimination against vulnerable market stakeholders must be factored into the regulatory motivation.[39] Regulation cannot cure all structural inequalities prevailing in market positioning, and flatten underlying market power asymmetries, but it can highlight for the most adversely affected and be mindful of and motivated by countering discrimination insofar as it is within regulatory reach, and as with bias, prevent both the data usage and its regulation from fuelling prevailing or emerging discrimination.

2. *Recognize and comply with established principles of ethical AI, big data use, and principled design* – Paramount among these principles for our purposes (as previously stated) will be
   • Accountability to the recipient community in terms they understand
   • Transparency when directed to authority/legitimacy and accountability of regulatory practice and outcomes
   • Fairness and harm avoidance when directed to good governance and data justice
   • Achieving human dignity and solidarity when directed to individual liberty/integrity
   Nominal ethical ascription and compliance when it comes to the operation of platform economies has failed to achieve equitable regulatory outcomes for vulnerable stakeholders. That does not mean ethics should be abandoned as a normative backbone for regulatory action. Rather, disruptive regulation adopts *an ethics plus* approach in its progress from

---

[39] Vulnerable is used here with specific connection to information deficit at key decision-sites in the marketizing of personal data.

ethics to action, where different regulatory techniques are complemented by an ethics 'backbone'.

3. *Promote data subject inclusion* – while many disruptive innovations tend to be exclusionist in the market by nature in that they protect their uniqueness for their knowhow asset valuing while seeking dominant market positioning, they usually require the broadest engagement across communities, and the more resilient examples offer inclusive, simple, and satisfactory opportunities for customer/seller conflict resolution such as in retail sales platforms. At a higher order, it is no longer enough, if customer/data subject preferences are to be maintained, for the shared data repositories and data traders to expect compliance emerging from ill-informed trust when many of the risks associated with data usage by disruptive innovation are not candidly revealed and openly negotiated.

In providing workable parameters for the proposed regulatory exercise, what follows focuses on tech/data applications as the *devices creating challenges*, and then on the challenges in themselves only insofar as they relate to the incursion of AI and the use of data. Through regulation it is personal data use challenges, not only technologies themselves (as is the criticism of 'trustworthy AI' discourse) that will be addressed by disruptive regulatory tools. More so, the contexts of AI applications and data usage are important considerations when diverting tech and data applications away from the problem and towards the solution. For instance, many pre-existing surveillance technologies/data use practices discussed in the snapshot to follow, for our purposes, have become more intrusive because of specious economic justifications surrounding disruptive technologies and their economies. Disruptive regulation demands that not only are the economic benefits of personal data reuse substantiated, but that the harmful social consequences of applying intrusive technologies, where emergent, are revealed.

DISRUPTING HARMFULNESS – SNAPSHOT OF DATA REUSE IN PLATFORM ECONOMIES

When it comes to focusing regulation against the harmful social consequences of disruptive innovation, regulatory 'disruption' suggests that rather than only being the objective of regulation and governance, AI and big data can be part of the regulatory armoury. For instance, AI-assisted data management in platform economies regularly conceals the nature and reuse of workers'/ customers' financial transaction data, but it also can be the technological medium for open banking and portability, fair-lending practices and more open algorithmic credit scoring.[40] AI can enable platform operators to garner surveillance and transactional data and to marketize it without the knowledge of the data subject. AI-assisted information loops can let vulnerable data subjects into the data business and empower their regulatory participation. Employing AI and big data to disrupt the ungoverned application and uses of AI and big data has not yet had any serious coverage in the regulation and governance policy thinking.

Using data reuse in platform economies as a snapshot of where disruptive regulation can be applied and how is instructive for this analysis. The case offers the specific connection between regulatory objectives countering the social harm caused by disruptive economies through the application of AI and data use in promoting social good outcomes such as informed data management, data marketing, accountability, and tighter data harvesting parameters. The regulatory theorizing underpinning this snapshot is that for human workers, regulation should enable social good, along with and above, market sustainability. This broad aspiration recognizes the alternative regressive neoliberal position taken by anyone arguing for the introduction of AI into the workplace primarily on profit and efficiency terms. This lobby usually rejects regulatory interference in favour of some compromised belief in data neutrality and the regulatory potency of competitive market forces. The intellectual poverty and the commercial duplicity of this position in platform economy oligopolies[41] once identified, can be countered by two arguments that move beyond humanist considerations of fairness alone:

- As the revaluation of platform-facilitated delivery and logistics services during the social distancing and movement restrictions of COVID-19 control policy reveal, depressed labour pricing and disempowered labour market participation are mechanically motivated internal market forces at work. A realistic understanding of labour revaluation relative to crisis utility is resisted by neoliberal pushback and is the market context in which disruptive regulatory intervention is advocated; and
- Human provision remains the bulk of platform service delivery and to ignore work-life quality in regulatory agendas is a short-sighted appreciation of market priorities, even when neoliberal discourse conceals

---

[40] Nydia Remolina, Aurelia Gurrea-Martínez, David Hardoon, and Yvonne Loh Ai-Chi, 'Regulatory Approaches to Consumer Protection in the Financial Sector and Beyond: Toward a Smart Disclosure Regime?' (May 25, 2020). SMU Centre for AI & Data Governance Research Paper No. 2020/05, Available at SSRN: https://ssrn.com/abstract=3609887 or http://dx.doi.org/10.2139/ssrn.3609887 accessed 19 April 2023.

[41] Frank Pasquale, 'Tech Platforms and the Knowledge Problem' (Summer 2018) *American Affairs* at 3.

'human capital' behind 'economic units' and conventional employment relationship disruption.[42] The answer is not to replace human labour but to humanize labour regulation.

AI impacts on labour markets by augmenting and/or substituting human capital in both mundane and specialist sites for decision-making.[43] Within most labour markets, the drivers for introducing AI are clearly based on profit: namely an expected reduced reliance on wage labour, and increased efficiency through mechanical predictability and reproductivity. AI technologies for managing and applying data in labour markets, outside facilitating market sustainability,[44] present risks for workers at the intersection of human agency and AI. Workers utilising platform communication markets are inextricably immersed in AI. The platform which masks employment arrangements behind 'independent service provision', sets rates of return, constructs transactions and sells on secondary data. These automations depend on big data, machine learning and computational interface. Platform technologies enhance service delivery and customer engagement but at the cost of depersonalizing the supply chain and giving market power to platform operators as exclusive agents in a variety of logistics transactions.

In the emerging context of platform facilitation, the labour market has developed in two ways. The first was an organic consequence of computerization in traditional economies, where organizations digitized their transactions

---

[42]   It is worth noting that recent judicial determinations in the UK and Europe have rejected the contention of platform operators that there is no employer/employee relationship between themselves and service providers. Such reversions to conventional employment expectations have brought welfare concessions and wage standardization from certain platform operators. 'Uber "willing to change" as drivers get minimum wage, holiday pay an pensions', *BBC News* (17 March 2021) https://www.bbc.com/news/business-56412397 accessed 19 April 2023.

[43]   Carl Benedict Frey, *The Technology Trap: Capital, Labor, and Power in the Age of Automation* (Princeton and Oxford: Princeton University Press, 2019). See also: Robin Teigland, Jochem van der Zande, Karoline Teigland and Sharhyar Siri 'The Substitution of Labor: From Technological Feasibility to Other Factors Influencing Job Automation' (2018) https://ssrn.com/abstract=3140364 accessed 8 August 2020.

[44]   Market sustainability in the context of this chapter is grounded in the observation that oligopolistic markets which operate on heavy stakeholder power disparities and exploit key vulnerable market players absent of capital interests will only continue to operate if the constituents of exploitation such as de-valued labour and regulatory distancing remain. As the COVID-19 crisis has shown with the new social valuing of some platform labour, externalities will impact on discriminatory sustainability.

and interactions with other market players. This phenomenon is not the interest of this analysis. Rather it is with the second:

> ...and potentially more consequential path of growth [which] began outside the traditional economy, as companies that have been born digital use the internet to usurp existing markets or create entirely new ones. Examples here involve e-commerce platforms, which have captured a growing share of the revenues once controlled by brick-and-mortar retail outlets; capital platforms or lodging, goods, and even machinery; service labor platforms for rides, household help, and caring labor; and video streaming and content platforms, which compete with broadcast, cable, and other media companies. The platform economy also encompasses social media firms such as Facebook and Instagram, which subsist on revenue from advertising and the sale of data, and internet service platforms such as Amazon Web Services, which provide the infrastructure on which other companies and platforms depend. As such, the platform economy represents an important and strategically consequential branch of global capitalism, not least because of the Schumpeterian creative destruction—or disruption, in the contemporary parlance—it has imposed across much of the economic landscape.[45]

Predatory capitalism[46] (which could be seen as the economic mores behind many disruptive economies that exploit undervalued labour) creates economic conditions that in turn feed on the vulnerabilities of many in its market reach. What is disrupted are conventional employer/employee arrangements, disengaging traditional worker protections, destabilizing bargaining power in any market/collective sense, and re-orienting even flexi-work[47] into employment environments devoid of predictability and certainty. If the wealth-creating benefits of disruptive economies are achieved by undervaluing vulnerable market activities, this is hardly market modernizing, but rather smacks of earlier discriminatory engagements between capital and labour. The new worker world is one re-imagined by a sanitised language of 'independent contracting', 'freelancing' and 'gigging' as some supplementary labour pass-time.[48] The tendency of such strained reinterpreting to further erode the

---

[45]   Steven Vallas and Juliet Schor, 'What do Platforms do? Understanding the Gig Economy' (2020) 46(1) *Annual Review of Sociology* 273–294 at 274–75.

[46]   Patrizia Zanoni, 'Labor Market Inclusion Through Predatory Capitalism? The "Sharing Economy," Diversity, and the Crisis of Social Reproduction in the Belgian Coordinated Market Economy' in Steven Vallas and Anne Kovalainen (eds) *Work and Labor in the Digital Age, Vol. 33* (Emerald Publishing Ltd, (2019) chap 6.

[47]   T Kumar and Kesari Jena, 'Capital vs. Digital Labor in the Post-industrial Information Age: A Marxist Analysis' (2020) 6(1) *Emerging Economy Studies* 50–60.

[48]   Kristine Kuhn,'The Rise of the "Gig Economy" and Implications for Understanding Work and Workers' (2016) 9(1) *Industrial and Organizational Psychology* 157–162.

dignity of the oppressed,[49] takes this thinking to its eventually perverted and now contested discourse.

Information deficits prevail across platform economies, and important data subjects such as service providers and customers are excluded from accessing the data they produce, and from knowing what and when their personal and transactional data is commodified. A lucrative market in the monetizing of secondary data, primarily the product of AI-assisted surveillance, is also debarred from worker/customer benefit.[50] In these circumstances, information (or its containment) presents two regulatory challenges:

1. general information closure. If workers do not have access to basic data which would indicate objective measures of labour value, they are in no position to construct informed representations on wages, conditions and work-life quality measures. Disempowerment in this form is exaggerated when the alternative performance measures such as customer satisfaction ratings are managed from the employer's perspective.[51]
2. intersections with automatically produced personal data (some that is monetised) over which the data subject has no control.

Both information-centred challenges:

*   Share a common characteristic, namely that the data/information deficit on which they rely disempowers vulnerable workers in crucial market interactions;
*   Determine data as a commodity with monetised value rather than as personal and essential to the integrity of the data subject and her privacy; and
*   Each are available for AI-assisted information technologies[52] to create data loops[53] that have potential to remedy information deficits and rebalance power asymmetries.

---

[49]   Jeremias Prassl, *Humans as a Service: The Promise and Perils of Work in the Gig Economy* (Oxford: Oxford University Press, 2018).

[50]   Shoshana Zuboff, *The Age of Surveillance Capitalism: The Fight for a Human Future at the New Frontier of Power* (New York: PublicAffairs, 2019).

[51]   Sarah O'Connor, 'Let gig workers control their data too', *Financial Times* (2018) https://www.ft.com/content/a72f7e56-3724-11e8-8b98-2f31af407cc8 accessed 8 August 2020.

[52]   By AI-assisted information technologies, we include the gamut of increasingly quotidian 'weak' AI/algorithmic processes that run in the background of technologies that we increasingly take for granted: social media news feeds, search engines, smartphones, and applications.

[53]   That is, sharing aggregated user data with platform users themselves.

Identifying these challenges to fair market participation as objects for regulation against which AI-assisted information management can be turned, offers opportunities to reflect on the importance of the disruptive regulatory paradigms which are detailed in the chapters to follow. Trust is absent in platform arrangements where workers and customers are kept in the dark about how their personal data is accessed and used once the nature of this practice is revealed. Particularly where it becomes obvious to service providers that they are distinctly disadvantaged in negotiations with the platforms concerning remuneration for services provided, too often the valuing of labour depends on information from which they are excluded. Digital self-determination would return trust not in the form of blind faith but rather a more mutualized recognition of personal data integrity through ensuring safe digital spaces for data to be democratized. Data emancipation in the direction of re-empowered data subjects will change the relationships that comprise disruptive innovation. Responsibility and sustainability will become the purposes communicated through the platform interface, and the 'profit above people' market mantra will be disrupted through the prioritizing of benefit for a wider domain of stakeholders.

To what extent can market dynamics be positively factored into disruptive regulation; or, are some of the myths about competitive natural selection exacerbated when disruptive innovation diverges from conventional market equalizers such as worker welfare? Putting faith in a derivative of market-centred self-regulation to address information deficits and power asymmetries demands critical reflection on the neoliberal assumption that markets provide a satisfactory regulatory paradigm, even where significant power displacement features. In practice, market regulatory potency is blunted by structural power asymmetries in existing labour market arrangements. These, as has been mentioned, are exacerbated by the slashing away of conventional market protections achieved by disruptive economies. As such, 'collective bargaining power' from the worker perspective is apocryphal, even illusory when labour is so individuated and undermined in any genuine compatible positioning. That said, as will be shown in the disruptive regulatory model to be proposed, informed participation as the essential conditions for sustainable self-regulation is designed to counter conventional regulatory capture, powerful to powerless,[54] and obviate any reliance on illusive market competition which the regulatory model cannot totally ensure. These condi-

---

[54] Jodi Short, 'Self-Regulation in the Regulatory Void: "Blue Moon" or "Bad Moon"?' (2013) 649(1) *The Annals of the American Academy of Political and Social Science* 22–34 https://doi.org/10.1177/0002716213485531 accessed 19 April 2023.

tions underpin the confidence in *inclusive, participatory self-regulation*.[55] This model will be detailed below.

AI-assisted information technologies presently enable platform providers with a distinct market advantage when surveillance data is commodified. These technologies harvest a mass of personal data during and beyond work-life environments as smart phone apps, and surveillance regimes offer data 24/7. Interestingly, the same technologies can be required through regulatory intervention to open information loops that will empower data subjects. Introducing AI to disrupt a fictitious bargaining market model for labour, however, will not be achieved through internal or external regulation alone. Even if information deficits are filled through information looping and vulnerable market players are empowered consequently, there needs to develop a regulatory counter-narrative in terms of motivation and outcomes, which values labour for its utility rather than through the market dominion of structurally inequitable technologized oligopolies. *AI for profit* market priorities exacerbate the fundamental power asymmetries underpinning labour devaluing and need to be challenged by regulatory motivations and outcomes

---

[55] Much of the literature on inclusive self-regulation comes from the education sector and focuses on the class-room context with diverse student demographics. For an interesting analysis connecting self-regulation in the workplace to issues of resiliency, see Mitchel Rothstein, Mathew McLarnon and Gillian King, 'The Role of Self-Regulation in Workplace Resiliency' (2016) 9(2) *Industrial and Organizational Psychology* 416–421' https://www.cambridge.org/core/journals/industrial-and-organizational-psychology/article/role-of-selfregulation-in-workplace-resiliency/6C40E0CFA646C53412587A02EF38F1CC accessed 19 April 2023. There is much more discussion of participatory self-regulation in the workplace, but it has a heavy focus on tripartism and ideas of stakeholder engagement in the more conventional state/employer/worker paradigm, see, e.g., Cynthia Estlund, 'Rebuilding the Law of the Workplace in an Era of Self-Regulation' (2005) 105 *Colum. L. Rev.* 319–404. This chapter is proposing something different – self-regulation wherein market players are included and participate in an empowered environment of information access. Self-regulation empowerment programmes again are not uncommon in a class-room setting, see, e.g., Timothy Cleary and Barry Zimmerman, 'Self-regulation Empowerment Program: A School-based Program to Enhance Self-regulated and Self-motivated Cycles of Student Learning' (2004) 41(5) *Psychology in the Schools* 537–550 https://knilt.arcc.albany.edu/images/7/74/Cleary_and_zimmerman.pdf accessed 19 April 2023. Empowerment is essential for inclusive participatory self-regulation. It is a novel approach in workplace engagement. The UN's Food and Agriculture Organisation has done some interesting work on self-regulation, information access and gender empowerment which resonates with our model's intentions, see, Sofie Isenberg, 'Investing in Information and Communication Technologies to Reach Gender Equality and Empower Rural Women', *Food and Agriculture Organization of the United Nations* (2019) http://www.fao.org/policy-support/tools-and-publications/resources-details/en/c/1195147/ accessed 19 April 2023.

which benefit vulnerable stakeholders. The more apparent unfairness of these asymmetries is a consequence of discourses that only monetarize the value of labour as a commodity within the deregulated production model, ignoring external and predominant themes of social good such as job security.

As discussed earlier in the rejection of any neoliberal/disruptive economy assertion that regulation hurts markets, the following section gives weight to the argument that responsible regulation designed to flatten power asymmetries and spread benefit will enhance market sustainability. Trusted market relationships depend on informed decision-making particularly where vulnerable stakeholders are included. Digital self-determination (see chap 3) returns essential choice to data subjects when managing their personal information (individually and in their communities). If trust and choice are apparent for those who up until now have been largely excluded from modern market benefit, then innovation will also be motivated to advance and ensure a more responsible apportioning of economic and social 'goods'.

REGULATION AS MARKET STIMULUS?

John Braithwaite's work on enforced self-regulation,[56] from which we have drawn inspiration, offers a balance between internally moderated and settled compliance measures, an information pathway for highlighting intentional and recurrent non-compliance, and external oversight for correction, repositioning and if necessary, penalty. On top of his model, a condition of automatic information sharing to lessen the internal power asymmetries that he recognizes in market settings where power is a consequence of organizational hierarchies is available through AI-assisted disruption (backed up by trust, digital self-determination and responsible innovation). In addition, the proposed regulatory model to follow harnesses technology which in its current form is responsible for information deficit, to provide a facility for information access and inclusion. It is assumed that AI-assisted decision-making and data-driven technologies[57] can support and enliven self-regulatory actors or forces by ensuring wider information sharing in a climate of openness and inclusion,

---

[56] John Braithwaite, 'Enforced Self-Regulation: A New Strategy for Corporate Crime Control' (1982) 80(7) *Michigan Law Review* 1466–1507.

[57] By AI-assisted decision-making and data-driven technologies, we refer to the gamut of increasingly quotidian 'weak' AI: algorithmic processes that run in the background of technologies that we increasingly take for granted: social media news feeds, search engines, smartphones, and applications.

through information access and clearer explanations of how algorithms impact employment decisions.[58]

In making this assertion it is not enough to hold that more information means more inclusion, more market power and more empowered regulatory influence. It is recognized that along with information enrichment, there is a need for enabling external market modifications that make more likely the involvement of better informed labour-force stakeholders to understand and participate in the decision processes and outcomes which are assisted by AI.[59] The technology needs a novel motivation for any new regulatory application to embed, and as such responsibility in a social as well as a market sense has to inform the innovation project. If trust is to underpin market sustainability, then the empowering of stakeholders by availing them of information needs to be fostered through individual and communal choices by data-subjects as to the trajectory of their personal data, within and beyond the market,

Via the inclusion in decision-making of a wider audience of interest, the regulatory project will be targeted at satisfying a greater range of legitimate regulatory beneficiaries.[60] Injecting AI-assisted information technologies into the regulatory frame, building up mutualized capacities and real opportunities for open-access to information, but with the specific intentions of revealing and making accountable AI-assisted employment decision-making and data collection, will meet some of the criticisms about capture and power imbalance that reverberate through the self-regulation literature.[61] In this way, AI is a regulatory medium with a regulatory focus.

There are dangers that the common absence of accountability and participatory democracy in some forms of self-regulation,[62] and market power

---

[58]   Later we discuss the mechanics of information looping, the possible resistance to it from platform providers, and the inducements for eventual compliance and participation. Although it also may be a necessary eventual precondition for a more balanced information playing field, we do not envisage formal algorithm explainability or auditing in this model.

[59]   There is not the time to detail the nature of AI information systems which we see as appropriate beyond building into surveillance technologies information loop capacities specifically framed for aggregated data access by workers and in some cases, customers.

[60]   In keeping with the 'social-good' regulatory motivation, vulnerable market participants are the subjects of inclusion and participation. It is assumed that powerful market players such as platform providers, already well serviced with employment data, will not require the model's assistance to participate.

[61]   See work by Short (2013) (n 54); Fiona Haines, *The Paradox of Regulation: What Regulation Can Achieve and What it Cannot* (Cheltenham: Edward Elgar Publishing, 2011).

[62]   Neil Gunningham and Joseph Rees, 'Industry Self-Regulation: An Institutional Perspective' (1997) 19(4) *Law & Policy* 363–414.

imbalance in labour valuing, will minimize the regulatory force and protective functions for labour at risk. Hence, the intention to include facilities for greater data access and inclusivity to counteract the negative influence of market power asymmetries.[63] In addition, through enforced self-regulation, there will be facilities for exposing non-compliance and seeking the assistance of an external regulatory presence.

EVALUATING THE REGULATION OF LABOUR ENGAGEMENT IN DIGITAL ECONOMIES – SNAPSHOT OF DISRUPTIVE OPPORTUNITIES IN SAFE DIGITAL SPACE V SURVEILLANCE CAPITALISM

Presently, with the broad acceptance of the digitalization of so many aspects of life, data and politics become increasingly intertwined. The dual communication/commodification frames of data infrastructures and pathways of data access now mean that big data is employed largely for commercial profit and data is viewed as a marketable 'thing'. It will be a battle to defeat this data-as-property predisposition, unless in exercising regulatory muscle, the strategy demarks safe digital space in which data-as-human interactions and their associated 'messaging' can be managed by data-subjects and their communities (see Chapter 3).

Shoshana Zuboff argues that this profit motivation for data access and use has led to a new form of capitalism – where big technology platforms extract of 'surplus data' in the form of behavioural data and trade on their proprietary analytical (predictive) value.[64] The platform, as such, sucks up profit while the user/service provider simply generates data to be sold on. Responding to this argument, Couldry and Mejias have argued that rather than marking a new stage of capitalism, data relations run parallel with labour relations in a market for data that can never be beyond the machine.[65] The once-observed dominant role of labour as the means of production in more conventional capitalist iterations, is now replaced by data commodification (through surreptitious surveillance technologies) as a primary market driver. What happens to

---

[63] These market power asymmetries resultant from forces for disembedding have led to the disputation over responsibility for anxiety and disaffection in market/social arrangements. They also are at the heart of wider regulatory challenges in ensuring better work-life quality for gig workers, which is not the focus of our present analysis.

[64] Shoshana Zuboff, *The Age of Surveillance Capitalism: The Fight for a Human Future at the New Frontier of Power* (1st edn, New York: Public Affairs, 2019).

[65] Nick Couldry and Ulises Mejias, *The Costs of Connection: How Data is Colonizing Human Life and Appropriating It for Capitalism* (Stanford: Stanford University Press, 2019).

worker engagement and work-life- quality as labour value retreats in the face of encompassing data commodification?

Unlike Couldry and Mejias's envisaging of data colonialism mirroring the function of historical colonialism, we are witnessing data profit outpacing labour profit in the market. In fact, the struggle to ensure that platform service providers receive fair value for their labour is only part of the initiative to flatten power asymmetries in the market. Regulation has to disrupt this one-sided commodification of personal data which at present occurs without any effective involvement from the data-subject. The parasitic market dynamic where data feeds from labour, is an essential regulatory challenge as much as is the equitable revaluing of labour. Enabling data-subjects through digital self-determination and responsibly redirecting innovation's energy towards an equitable spread of market benefit are necessary features of disruptive regulation pitted against one-sided data commodification.

Data commodification for exclusionist profit needs the datafication of human experience[66] to grow as a market commodity, and to be transformed from 'personal' to 'business' conceptualizing. To advance this market phenomenon, data extraction necessitates the mining of human experience, which is in turn rationalized into data messages, abstract from human life and thereby something which is exchangeable.[67] The digitalization and datafication of human activity as assets thereby contribute to a significant transformation in value creation that marks the platform labour-capital relationship. Disruptive regulation will require of this relationship at least equal recognition of the market significance of power dispersal and equitable benefit for social good and market sustainability.

Out from these observations there are disempowering market influences operating in tandem. The first is surveillance capitalism, extracting data from life experience and commodifying it for market exchange. The second draws from Benanav's observations of a deepening economic stagnation that manifests as mass underemployment, being a natural consequence of the neoliberal wealth creation cycle but blamed as the result of globalization.[68] The combined effect of these regressive forces sees innovation to the detriment of vulnerable stakeholders in the market, through the extraction of data for profit and exploiting devalued labour in the context of alternative underemployment.

---

[66]   Viktor Mayer-Schönberger and Kenneth Cukier, *Big data: A Revolution That Will Transform How We Live, Work, and Think* (Houghton Mifflin Harcourt, 2014).

[67]   Nick Couldry and Ulises Mejias, *The Costs of Connection: How Data is Colonizing Human Life and Appropriating It for Capitalism* (Stanford: Stanford University Press, 2019).

[68]   Aaron Benanav, 'Automation and the Future of Work – I' (2019) 119 *New Left Review* 5–38.

Vulnerable stakeholders are deprived of market benefit from their datafication and labour both by decreasing labour's share of income through concentrating returns to those at the top of platform management *and* by furthering the capacity for breaking jobs into segmented tasks and thus *adding* to what Graham and Anwar have identified as the planetary labour market.[69] Tasks are reduced to sub-labour forms which are disaggregated while still connected to more consolidated labour objectives. Disaggregation in this way further fractures sustainable wage labour by making workers dependent on what the platform choses to commercialize, a decision which is driven by profit and not by socially embedding market relations.

Amir Anwar critically reviewed the consequences of disaggregation and alienation:

> The contemporary gig economy represents the latest manifestation of the restructuring of capitalism...advancements made in digital technologies have generated new divisions of labour, defined as the specialisation or separation of tasks between different types of workers...on platforms, commodification of labour power is made possible as thousands of workers compete globally for digital tasks...for Marx, alienation of workers is at the heart of capitalist production... Alienation is even more present in the way the global gig economy is organised and controlled. Job descriptions on platforms are often vague and unspecified, the client is looking for workers with the lower rates rather than a certain skill set. Workers do not know who their client is. The fact that workers are competing for short-term gigs like these means that they have less incentive to know what they are creating, for who and to what purposes. Thus, the more work they do, the more alienated they become...[70]

If these observations hold true also for AI engineers, technicians, and other professionals throughout the AI ecosystem it may be little more than wishful thinking to talk of principled design as the preferred regulatory paradigm ensuring responsible data use. The attribution and distribution of ethical responsibility for AI technology and algorithm applications of big data depend on recognizing and mediating external market strain brought about through neoliberal exclusionist wealth creation as the regulatory purpose.[71]

The symbiotic commercial relationship between data marketing and digital platform employment arrangements and data reuse highlights information

---

[69] Graham Mark and Mohammad Anwar, 'The Global Gig Economy: Towards a Planetary Labour Market?' (2019) 24(4) *First Monday*.

[70] Mohammad Anwar, 'How Marx predicted the worst effects of the gig economy more than 150 years ago', *NS Tech, New Statesman* (2018) https://tech.newstatesman.com/guest-opinion/karl-marx-gig-economy.

[71] Mark Findlay and Josephine Seah, 'Data Imperialism: Disrupting Secondary Data in Platform Economies Through Participatory Regulation' (May 29, 2020). SMU Centre for AI & Data Governance Research Paper No. 2020/06.

deficits, surreptitious data acquisitions, and irresponsible data commodification that have become institutional features of work-life-quality for vulnerable service providers. There also need to be elements for behavioural change in disruptive regulation strategies. Data commodification enjoys monetary value that is created secondary to original service provision, either emerging from surveillance technologies at places of employment, or through the collection and selling of client/service-provider data through third-party brokers. Just by one's interaction with – or perhaps in proximity to – digital platforms and their surveillance capacities, data is produced and potentially commodified. Van Doorn has pointed out that through their production of raw data, gig workers engage in 'dual value production' in the following manner:

> …besides extracting rent *from* each transaction they orchestrate, platforms can also extract data *about* these transactions, which means that gig workers can likewise be understood to provide an 'informational service' to platforms… [as such] the monetary value produced by the service provided is augmented by the use and speculative value of data produced before, during, and after service provision.[72]

Inverting worker productivity from labour to data, and revaluing labour worth against data marketization, is the context from which the regulatory effort needs to reposition vulnerable market stakeholders centrally within this new commercial dynamic. At the very least, if data, compulsorily extracted and unaccountably commodified, remains out of the reach of say work-place bargaining, then any regulatory focus on labour productivity alone will miss touching the reality of new market arrangements. Add to this anonymous human engagement across platform service provision, the human/machine interface (each dehumanizing) and the position of workers in any counter-regulatory frame becomes an essential consideration in its potential impact in reasserting labour value and worker integrity. This counter-regulatory frame (disruptive regulation) builds from rocky market foundations. Trust cannot be even contemplated between platform operators and service providers/customers when transaction data is sold on without notification of the data subjects. The possibility, therefore, for digital self-determination is beyond the regulator's reach without employing data use and management processes/technology that informs vulnerable stakeholders about the way their data is monetised. If this information is made available then essential market participants, presently excluded from the benefits of innovation, become partners in a responsible innovation project.

---

[72] Nicholas van Doorn, N. 'On Data Assets and Meta-platforms. Platform Labor', (2019, July 9) https://platformlabor.net/blog/on-data-assets-and-meta-platforms accessed 20 April 2023.

Recognizing automation, dispersal and disempowerment, regulatory policy makers need to craft styles that integrate currently isolated market players (workers in particular) through information emancipation and the creation of safe digital spaces to participate effectively in accountability frames. The aim here is that with access to more and better information, the participation of data-subjects in the regulatory enterprise will more equitably apportion data management and consequential benefit, and thereby open greater appreciations of their data value and their personal integrity.

Service providers and customers (data-subjects) in platform arrangements are presently the largely passive objects of what is known; they are excluded from any further benefit through the commodified valuation of their data by conscious veils of ignorance thrown around their market positioning by the platforms.[73] Reflecting on empowering forms of disruptive regulatory engagement in such a market of data exclusivity and adapting their benefits to a power-fractured platform economy will require regulation at the point that other market players acquire data about transactional behaviours and commercially act on that knowledge. The problem facing conventional organized solidarity movements for labour welfare and consumer advocacy regarding power imbalance in such contexts is that the scope of ignorance about digitization goes much further than the individual worker/customer and their market positioning. As such the universal interests of members in a labour organization must also run in parallel to efforts recognizing and protecting the individual integrity of personal data.

From employing digital infrastructure, disruptive regulations turn AI-assisted information technology towards the purpose of flattening exclusionist platform power imbalance through the inclusion of aware data-subjects. As previously suggested, this would represent a positive regulatory development if such incorporation was for the purposes of illuminating the decision-making process that comprises the interface between human agency and AI data use.

In parallel with political empowerment through technological augmentation to regulatory purposes, Morozov furthered Mayer-Schönberger and Ramge's

---

[73] Nick Srnicek *Platform Capitalism* Oxford: Policy (2016); See also Martin Kenney and John Zysman, 'Work and Value Creation in the Platform Economy' in Steven Vallas and Anne Kovalainen (eds.) *Work and Labor in the Digital Age, Vol. 33* (Emerald Publishing Limited, 2018) chap 1.

identification of 'feedback data'[74] as a future site of empowerment politics[75] by arguing that:

> We need to widen the scope of the concept and consider 'feedback infrastructure' itself: the ownership and operation of the means of producing 'feedback data' are at least as important as the question of who owns the data itself. The crucial battles ahead will involve the role of this 'feedback infrastructure' in the reinvention of the political projects of both left and right.[76]

The concept of transactional openness via feedback infrastructure is more appealing for disruptive regulation than contested arguments about data ownership. The chapter that explores digital self-determination will not entertain concepts of property and sovereignty in an age where data access is fast becoming the market aspiration and the potential wealth creator. An atmosphere of access is ripe for persuading those who might otherwise jealously guard data for ownership considerations, to enable access as evidence of their claim to responsible data use. As such, a more productive regulatory discussion moves away from confronting predatory and exclusive data ownership/control, to being involved in the active shaping of data dissemination. In this discourse, it becomes more impactful to expose resistance against data feedback, rather than engaging in debate over data ownership/control as the primary regulatory expression, and instead to create a data-subject-focused impetus for data openness. This is not an argument for the removal of barriers currently existing to regulate unencumbered flows of data,[77] but to highlight that in data assemblages,[78] there are choices to be made in the conceptualization of data and its subsequent movement from one set of social actors to another, which are implicated in entrenched power distributions. As has been argued by others

---

[74]   Viktor Mayer-Schönberger V. and Tomas Ramge (2018) *Reinventing Capitalism in the Age of Big Data* (New York: Basic Books, 2018).

[75]   A concept that encompasses social, economic and political empowerment usually through organizational inclusion, but in this situation, more as a result of regulatory intervention with power dispersal as its political purpose.

[76]   Evgeny Morozov, 'Digital Socialism? The Calculation Debate in the Age of Big Data' (2019) 116/117 *New Left Review* 33–67.

[77]   To provide participants with masses of personalized or non-aggregated data would open up real privacy and integrity concerns which would undermine the success of efforts for information looping.

[78]   Rob Kitchin and Tracey Lauriault, 'Towards Critical Data Studies: Charting and Unpacking Data Assemblages and Their Work' in Jim Thatcher, Joseph Eckert and Andrew Shears (eds) *Thinking Big Data in Geography: New Regimes, New Research* (Lincoln: University of Nebraska Press, 2014) Chap 1.

about data valuing, 'data capture and its use to meet specific needs or interest are what makes it valuable; not data itself'.[79]

It is preferable to shift the grounds for discussion away from boundary formations around data – data as a form of property or a thing over which sovereignty can dominate – to looking at the ways in which data friction[80] might be enhanced or smoothed out when market transactions are increasingly datafied. The notion of friction points for enlivening new attitudes and approaches to ethics in regulation is elaborated in Chapter 4. When this process is the norm, a more responsible regime for innovation will depend on data access not clandestine in achievement, but open to data-subjects in the hope that more and more data will be used when responsible access is implicit.

If safe data spaces can be achieved through and for responsible data access, then trust bonds metering data flow will become a market necessity as well as a regulatory imperative.

INCLUSIVE, PARTICIPATORY SELF-REGULATION – DISRUPTIVE REGULATION AS THE WAY FORWARD?

Moving from information deficits and market power asymmetries which are exacerbated by algorithmic obscurity and platform containment, important steps in activating the disruptive regulatory enterprise provide:

(a) access for vulnerable stakeholders/data-subjects to essential information managed and manipulated by data harvesters;

(b) incentives, via increased responsible access, to those currently monetising secondary data, to participate in and contribute towards inclusive participatory self-regulation, in the form of digital self-determination;

(c) motivation through responsible innovation to move away from secretive and combative data protection posturing into more open data sharing as the precursor to regulatory responsibility; and to ensure that;

(d) the regulatory project progresses along a continuum — from command and control to enforced self-regulation — as the benefits of the latter become clear to those who presently oppose regulatory openness.[81]

---

[79] Ashlin Lee and Petra Cook, 'The Myth of the "data-driven" Society: Exploring the Interactions of Data Interfaces, Circulations, and Abstractions' (2019) 14(1) *Sociology Compass* https://doi.org/10.1111/soc4.12749 accessed 20 April 2023.

[80] Jo Bates, 'The Politics of Data Friction' (2018) 74(2) *Journal of Documentation* 412–429 https://doi.org/10.1108/JD-05-2017-0080 accessed 20 April 2023.

[81] Mark Findlay 'Regulating Regulation—Who Guards the Guardian', in *Contemporary Challenges in Regulating Global Crises* (London: Palgrave Macmillan, 2019) chap. 9.

It is anticipated that in the first stage of the disruptive regulatory model applied to platform economy clandestine data reuse, there will be impediments to information openness while data harvesters are convinced of the benefits of consequential data access through more responsible innovation. These impediments are technical and operational:

- Locating and identifying automatically produced personal data on regulatory recipients (primarily vulnerable workers and their customers);
- Respecting data privacy/integrity if the data is not anonymous in its feedback form or not aggregated in bulk;
- Introducing AI-assisted technologies to notify regulatory recipients of data production, storage and use;
- Creating convenient paths of open access which recognize commercially sensitive data that may attach to automatically produced personal data;
- Ensuring internal privacy protections covering the identity of data subjects;
- Educating regulatory recipients in the use and utility of AI-assisted information technologies and their data pathways;
- Enabling regulatory recipients with simple tools to analyse the significance of automatically produced personal data; and in the spirit of enforced self-regulation;
- To activate and enable an 'honest broker' third party/agency to ensure that conditions covering access are complied with.

Arguments about data ownership and who bears the responsibility and cost for establishing this access and information framework will need to be settled at the 'command and control' end of the regulatory model (between a relevant state agency and the platform managers/administrators). Harking back to an earlier section of the chapter, *the responsibility to build in regulatory strategies to avoid harm and misuse rests first with powerful data harvesters.* The issue of resourcing participation will need the processes of arbitration so that fundamental disputes have an orderly and legitimate resolution at the hands of an honest third party, data steward or data trust. [82] Once trust relationships replace suspicion and contestation and digital self-determination is embedded, then third-party intervention will recede, and safe digital spaces come to the fore.

---

[82]	Chris Reed and Irene Ng, 'Data Trusts as an AI Governance Mechanism' (2019) https://papers.ssrn.com/sol3/papers.cfm?abstract_id=3334527 accessed 20 April 2023; see also Sylvie Delacroix and Neil Lawrence, 'Bottom-up Data Trusts: disturbing the "one size fits all" Approach to Data Governance' (2019) 9(4) *International Data Privacy Law* 236–252. https://doi.org/10.1093/idpl/ipz014 accessed 20 April 2023.

In present day platform environments, the adoption and construction of information infrastructures such as those identified above concentrate and polarize power in the hands of the platform operators, while regulators and their regulated entities are largely excluded from these information pathways. In the initial stage of the regulatory enterprise, the problems facing effective engagement with disempowered market players in participatory self-regulation boil down to the likely 'capture' of ill-informed and data-starved stakeholders by more data powerful participants (including external regulators). Capture is not only a consequence of obscuring rather than revealing the nature, purpose, and processes of data, but also will arise if regulatory participants do not understand and share the regulatory purpose of information emancipation. Opening up data access in a manner which encourages shared participation and trusting inclusion requires creating an information infrastructure which flattens structural imbalances by encouraging bottom-up data management models.[83] Obviously this is a more than a market structure issue and will rely on the extent to which digital self-determination can displace power over data access. As a pre-condition in its development the information access technology and pathways need to reflect a more equitable user-driven format.[84] The disruptive regulatory model will need to counter the current market reality that algorithmic intervention adds cash to the pockets of the information governors. The counter message against data as an exclusive commodity is a more universal and widespread recognition of the need, and ancillary benefits offered from revealing and repositioning automatically produced personal information from market abuse and data-subject discrimination, to data-subject management and responsible access.[85] Once this message has been grounded in the regulatory enterprise, then other key players in market productivity (vulnerable regulatory recipients) need a place in an informed and inclusive decision-making interface, that will be the dispute resolution phase of the disruptive regulatory model. Only then will inclusive self-regulation grow to its potential for market power dispersal. So that this process will take root, state agencies as licensing authorities, for instance, could impose external conditions on market entry

---

[83] Delacroix and Lawrence, ibid.

[84] An initial challenge lies in the current market reality that the platform providers claim ownership of the personal data automatically produced through commercial and surveillance technologies, and will resist any possibility that its value as a market commodity may be reduced through more open access. Data ownership determinations must not be a prohibitive pre-condition to the regulatory enterprise.

[85] Mor Bakhoum, Beatriz Conde Gallego, Mark-Oliver Mackenrodt and Gintare Surblytė-Namavičienė, *Personal Data in Competition, Consumer Protection and Intellectual Property Law: Towards a Holistic Approach?* (MPI Studies on Intellectual Property and Competition Law, Vol. 28) (2018) Springer.

– making this dependent on arrangements for bottom-up information management and inclusive operational decision-making.

Today, not only are certain platform operators denying data-subjects a place at the decision-making table, but there is also attendant exclusion from information as a facility and a function for inclusive self-regulation, and thereby repudiating the need for a table around which to discuss grievances. Above this power-grab is the appetite for surveilling users as valuable data mines. If datafication is driving such surveillance systems and contributing to information asymmetries, then it needs also to be productive for data-subjects and self-regulatory mechanisms by 'feed[ing] such data back to users, enabling them to orient themselves in the world'.[86]

To complement a move away from regulatory elitism and myopia focused on the profitability of irresponsible innovation and towards participant inclusion through information access, important external players such as government agencies, labour organizations, consumer advocates and data rights groups must ensure that the data-subject is institutionally included in the regulatory process: both in its crafting and implementation. These are a priori external market requirements if information access is to contribute to regulatory empowerment as this analysis predicts.

CHAPTER DIRECTIONS

As already foreshadowed, the first interest of this book will be in 'disrupting' conventional regulation and governance discourses concerning AI and big data. For instance, the analysis will not confine its consideration of trust as regulation to some abstract or universalized context in which technology operates or is received, or some outcome resulting out of ethical compliance.[87] Instead we see trust as a regulatory agent/process whereby AI operating within communities can only be legitimated (and its behaviours managed or changed) where strong bonds of trust between humans and machines are in operation. In addition, the essence of locating AI within communities and thereby participating in purposes which those communities deem valuable and sustainable internalizes considerations of ethical decision-making within particular com-

---

[86] Helen Kennedy, Thomas Poell and Jose van Dijck, 'Data and Agency' (2015) 2(2) *Big Data & Society* https://doi.org/10.1177/2053951715621569 accessed 20 April 2023.

[87] Mark Findlay and Willow Wong, 'Trust and Regulation: An Analysis of Emotion' (June 1, 2021). SMU Centre for AI & Data Governance Research Paper No. 05/2021, available at SSRN: https://ssrn.com/abstract=3857447 or http://dx.doi.org/10.2139/ssrn.3857447 accessed 20 April 2023.

munal morality, enabling trust/distrust to be measured and manipulated for regulatory determinations.[88]

The disruptive force of *trust as regulation* challenges the asymmetrical power dynamics between data-collectors and data-subjects whose personal data are collected, monetized, and reused in the production cycle of AI technologies. The disruptive characteristics of AI ethics only enter the picture when key decision parties in the AI ecosystem can effectively counter ongoing ethics-washing initiatives, where ethical principles are used as convenient sources of positive corporate branding. The 'disruptive' side of applying AI ethics, as a regulatory instrument to rebuild shared trust, pushes AI actors to make decisions with community benefits in mind. Therein lies the potential to disrupt the status quo and redistribute decision-making power to extend ethical responsibilities horizontally across the whole AI ecosystem. All this is achieved by directing ethics to challenge rather than authorise responsible innovation.

When it comes to the discussion of data management, our development of digital self-determination is a radical departure from rights on one hand, and commodification on the other. Digital self-determination identifies the need to create safe digital spaces in which data subjects can negotiate the management of their data, recognizing communal responsibility and not just individual interests. This way of thinking imagines the power differentials that underpin the place of data in digital societies and endeavours to empower vulnerable players in data markets to have a voice in the management of personal data and its eventual uses.

The disruptive dimension of digital self-determination is through recognizing data power asymmetries often passed over in more impotent rights aspirations, or by trying to return data to silos when the concept of data transgression has morphed into mass data sharing. Instead of pretending rights protect and data can be safely segregated, DSD looks back to who initially created the data and who, therefore, should predominate in its management. Digital self-determination is a fundamentally disruptive regulator because the data subject is principally empowered by requiring more powerful stakeholders to relinquish and redirect their power for the sake of mutualizing responsible access interests. According to DSD power is not dispersed through contests over rights, or litigating laws, or compliance with best practice, in claiming to give data subjects a seat at the regulatory table. Instead, because the data

---

[88] Mark Findlay and Willow Wong, 'Kampong Ethics' in Urvashi Aneja (ed), *Reframing AI Governance: Perspectives from Asia* (Digital Futures Lab; Konrad-Adenauer-Stiftung 2022) https://www.ai-in-asia.com/06-kampong-ethics accessed 13 August 2022

market and access innovation climate changed from over-emphasising data security to facilitating data access, there is a window of opportunity to create a self-regulatory model that is DSD based on inclusion and empowered participation. All this is achieved by changing who governs data and how it is valued.

The final case-study on ethical frictions goes back into the AI/big data ecosystems and explores attribution and distribution of responsible practices from the grassroots and across all key decision sites in AI pipelines. This work attempts to take the principled approach to AI creation and deployment off the boardroom wall and to test how responsibility has reality for different key operatives and teams within the process from concept to application. Organizational communication strategies (confronting blockages and blind spots) are the empirical testbed for whether responsibility in the broadest sense can be located and activated in AI ecosystems. Ethics is proposed not to solve governance challenges but to act as a friction point for revealing those influences and pressures that make principled design and responsible deployment difficult.

Trust bonds, communal location, self-determination, and ecosystem responsibility build a wider regulatory tapestry against which practical examples of regulatory need and current failure will be met with a new way of seeing AI and big data in the service of social good. Only then will it be confidently asserted that AI can assist in achieving the UN Sustainable Development Goals and addressing contemporary crises such as pandemic abatement and diminishing the negative impacts of global warming.

AI governance is more than trustworthy technology. It means locating AI within communities as positive contributors to social good. AI in community is compatible with the maintenance of sustainable trust bonds. The good governance outcomes are achieved through collaboration by multiple actors with a common understanding of AI and humans working together to achieve sustainable communities. The analysis will introduce research into governing the AI ecosystem and mass data sharing. It looks at challenges to AI governance met through governance by people. Governance should not be the domain of technology alone but requires a focus on how AI relates to pressing community needs. If this can be achieved, then we are not only concerned with governing AI but how AI can assist in wide projects of good governance.

2. Trust as regulation[1]

By Willow Wong

INTRODUCTION

Whether artificial intelligence (AI) technologies[2] can promote human dignity, social good, and justice for individuals and societies is a recurring question that surfaces in situations of global crises. The COVID-19 pandemic has witnessed a drastic erosion of trust among citizens and towards public institutions, resulting in the devaluation of scientific truths and collective action in the mainstream zeitgeist.[3] The adverse effects can be seen through inefficiency in implementing evidence-based pandemic control and prevention policies, which spiral outwards to destabilize the government's political legitimacy on a broader scale.[4] At the same time, however, there is greater recognition that effective responses to major global crises – with consequences unconstrained by geographies, market economies, or jurisdictions – will likely require multilateral cooperation among the local, regional, and global communities. The UNESCO World Philosophy Day 2021, with its central theme of 'intercultural philosophy for peace and sustainability in the time of crisis', is one of many existing efforts to encourage a deeper embedding of local value systems into

[1] This research is supported by the National Research Foundation, Singapore under its Emerging Areas Research Projects (EARP) Funding Initiative. Any opinions, findings and conclusions or recommendations expressed in this material are those of the author(s) and do not reflect the views of National Research Foundation, Singapore.

[2] Artificial Intelligence (AI) refers mainly to weak AI operating in spheres where public opinion is predicted as a critical factor in determining the success of its widespread adoption (e.g., smartphones, facial recognition technologies, content recommendation algorithms). The mention of AI technologies in this analysis also extends to big data's role in enhancing AI systems' performances.

[3] Ava Kofman, 'Bruno Latour, the Post-Truth Philosopher, Mounts a Defense of Science' *The New York Times* (25 October 2018) https://www.nytimes.com/2018/10/25/magazine/bruno-latour-post-truth-philosopher-science.html accessed 8 April 2021.

[4] Olivier Bargain and Ulugbek Aminjonov, 'Trust and Compliance to Public Health Policies in Times of COVID-19' (2020) 192 *Journal of Public Economics* 104316.

large-scale decision-making models and high-level regulatory considerations.[5] For global partnerships in AI governance to be meaningful and inclusive, strong participation from under-represented communities is required to leverage diverse community-centric ethics to tackle common challenges posed by AI technologies.

Often missing from governance spheres and regulatory discourse, the voices of data-subjects – that is, people who will likely experience the unintended consequences of AI pervasiveness in their lives – rarely hold concrete influence over AI policy making activities.[6] Similarly, the social drivers of community anxieties or negative perceptions towards potential disruptions triggered by technological innovations – of which AI counts as one of many other tools – remain largely unaddressed in the abstract languages of AI ethics. Even if these frameworks acknowledge the contextual factors at play in the regulatory environment, what is unchallenged is the central seat of power from which a small number of big tech companies and government entities exert control over the regulatory processes. More specifically, recent calls for expert and technologists to join forces in engineering 'trustworthy AI' has positioned public trust as a regulatory panacea to bring AI further into community living spaces.[7]

Against this backdrop, this book chapter posits the central role of community trust in activating healthy disruption to the mainstream regulatory approach towards AI and big data. The social conditions of trust, as part of formulating community-centric ethics, effectively channels public distrust as the disruptive regulatory force to redistribute decision-making powers away from existing powerholders (i.e., those responsible for overseeing AI creation and operation) in favour of civic voices (i.e., human recipients of AI tech-

---

[5] 'Celebration of World Philosophy Day' (*UNESCO*) https://events.unesco.org/event/?id=4146300908&lang=1033 accessed 9 February 2022.

[6] Data subjects are community members or the general public whose personal data are collected to inform the design and operation of AI technologies. This includes situations where data collection takes place even when the public members are not the targeted end-users of the AI system, but nevertheless come into casual encounters with such technologies operating in community spaces. As such, the term 'human recipients' of AI technologies are also used in this analysis to describe these more generic scenarios, where the average member of the public may have limited powers to resist against the consequences of AI roll-out into their everyday lives.

[7] Balázs Bodó and Heleen Janssen, 'Here Be Dragons – Maintaining Trust in the Technologized Public Sector' (Social Science Research Network 2021) SSRN Scholarly Paper ID 3868208 https://papers.ssrn.com/abstract=3868208 accessed 11 February 2022.

nologies).[8] On top of a clear emphasis on AI value alignment – matching AI capabilities with community needs via co-creation pathways – the disruptive force of *trust as regulation* also challenges the asymmetrical power dynamics between data-collectors and data-subjects whose personal data are collected, monetized, and reused in the production cycle of AI technologies.[9]

In proposing an alternative ethical decision-making framework, this chapter envisions the value of leveraging community participation to negotiate the AI futures unfolding in their local contexts. Crucial to the revival of social bondedness is the broader recognition of human dignity calls for any regulatory action to look beyond commercial incentives to decide whether to integrate or prohibit AI technological products from a targeted community of people. In other words, this spirit of solidarity, shared fate, and togetherness sits above the profit incentives of the AI marketplace. Positioning community members as a central driver of the AI governance agenda will likely manifest differently across distinct policy and regulatory environments. As a starting point, however, this chapter suggests inviting public scrutiny over the types of technologies deemed acceptable by the values, norms, and standards most salient to the specific host communities. Core questions of AI governance include:

- Are there clear 'winners' and 'losers' among all parties implicated in the AI roll-out?
- Can all members of the AI ecosystem, especially data subjects, participate in decision-making processes?[10] Whose voices might be excluded, and by what types of barriers?
- What actions or adjustments are needed to ensure ethical responsibilities are appropriately distributed across the AI decision-making pipeline?

Much of the answers to the open-ended questions above depend on members of the public to negotiate, as a collective, the basics of *how*, *where*, and *why* AI technologies should be introduced to diverse environments involving different demographics of society. As such, the regulatory effort to ensure AI operations do not harm existing community interests traces back to the foundations of social and institutional trust. As this chapter will continue to demonstrate, the calibration of community trust (or lack thereof) refers to sourcing public

---

[8]   Sherry R Arnstein, 'A Ladder of Citizen Participation' (2019) 85 *Journal of the American Planning Association* 24.

[9]   Mabel Choo and Mark Findlay, 'Data Reuse and Its Impacts on Digital Labour Platforms' (Social Science Research Network 2021) SSRN Scholarly Paper 3957004 https://papers.ssrn.com/abstract=3957004 accessed 25 May 2022.

[10]   The AI ecosystem refers to the key decision sites hosting different teams or stakeholders involved in the pipeline of how AI technologies are designed, developed, and eventually deployed.

sentiments toward AI technologies; the regulatory function of this exercise emerges when AI creators, sponsors, and regulators are pushed to address public discontentment due to the weight of community trust upon the success or failure of AI roll-out.[11]

The scope of consideration outlined above clarifies that this chapter will not focus on which ethical values or principles are the best choices for AI governance, even if they are used to guide the conscientious deployment of AI technologies into community spaces. What is arguably more important, however, is ensuring that AI ethics can exert influence over context-specific decision-making processes. As a regulatory instrument, then, AI ethics and AI governance initiatives must attend to the normative conditions enabling people-to-people trust – from which trust perceptions towards AI technologies are shaped and formed.[12] Tracing the causal chain of human decisions that may erode social cohesion in the community will also reveal where abstract ethical principles might lose operational effectiveness, as a victim of negative perceptions and perverse externalities. In short, this chapter shows how *trust as regulation* can revive the practical operations of ethical decision-making in AI governance. Building community trust also disrupts tokenistic forms of public consultation exercises, instead striving towards meaningful rehabilitation of strained social ties, strengthening people-to-people trust, and preserving social togetherness amidst rapid technological change.

This chapter will proceed in three sections. The first section, 'Community and Ethics', critiques mainstream iterations of AI ethical frameworks before proposing an alternative model geared towards building public acceptance of AI technologies. This community-centric framework identifies the requirements for harmonious AI-human coexistence and connects AI ethics to this task. The second section, 'Emotions', explores the influences of affectivity that undermine the effectiveness of abstract ethical principles. The requirements for AI governance to reconcile rational explanations of AI safety with affective-driven public trust judgements towards AI technologies are

---

[11]   AI decision parties refer to the entities with varying levels of power to contribute to the conception and creation of AI technologies upstream *and* influence their deployment into intended community spaces further downstream. This includes the AI creators, engineers, private and public funding bodies, government agencies endorsing AI technologies, elected representatives overseeing AI regulation, lawmakers, etc.

[12]   For avoidance of doubt, the emphasis on the regulatory importance of resolving areas of community distrust is not to be confused with other motivations to eliminate voices of dissent. As a counterweight to human propensity to trust, intentional application of epistemic scepticism can promote healthy public reasoning to determine why the community chooses to extend (or withdraw) their trust towards an entity. It is, therefore, not the goal of this analysis to advocate for the elimination of all possible sources of distrust in society as a successful regulatory outcome.

revealed. The final section of this chapter outlines trust as a regulatory force that provokes behavioural changes in the key players of AI governance. The conceptions of trust are summarized to offer insights into how trust calibration can be applied to activate community-centric processes to govern AI on local, regional, and global levels. Lastly, a visual representation is also presented to show the causal interplay between social bonding, community, ethics, emotions, and trust as critical components in the AI governance sphere.

1. COMMUNITY AND ETHICS

This section argues that mainstream AI ethical frameworks generally fail to reflect diverse systems of thinking across communities worldwide. An alternative ethical decision-making model is proposed to connect AI design and deployment choices with the various norms, values, and standards specific to the host community, to cultivate public receptivity towards AI. Contrarily, AI deployment into host environments without prior community engagements carries the risk of community apathy, low trust, or adverse public receptivity. AI roll-out might cause public suspicion and rejection, even if the software systems have been rigorously tested, audited, and certified functionally safe by private or public entities. Establishing the disconnection between 'community' and 'ethics' in this section paves the way for later discussions on the regulatory barriers posed by trust perceptions (section 2) and trust building in the community (section 3).

1.1   Limitations of Ethical Principles and Abstract Certification Frameworks

Questions of what makes AI technologies 'trustworthy' or 'ethical', and the answers provided, will draw from the judgements of the individuals, other community members, and the institutions relevant to such community contexts. The average person's perception of an AI system may draw from their prior knowledge and broader public sentiments on the risks and benefits promised by such technologies. Yet dominant forms of AI ethics featuring principles[13] and certifications[14] are usually jargon-heavy, excluding public

---

[13]   Jessica Morley and others, 'From What to How: An Initial Review of Publicly Available AI Ethics Tools, Methods and Research to Translate Principles into Practices' (2020) 26 *Science and Engineering Ethics* 2141.

[14]   Sergio Genovesi and Julia Maria Mönig, 'Acknowledging Sustainability in the Framework of Ethical Certification for AI' (2022) 14 *Sustainability* 4157.

understanding of the fundamental questions that underpin external motivations for AI roll-out in their locality:

- What purpose does this AI technology serve?
- Who is advocating for its (widespread or limited) usage?
- Where and how is this AI technology used, and for how long?
- What happens to the personal data collected during the operation of this AI technology?
- Who will be advantaged or otherwise become disadvantaged by AI roll-out?
- How does the decision pipeline protect those vulnerable to AI's potential social impacts?

These considerations can bring additional transparency and accountability to high-level governance decisions made in the AI ecosystems, but they are not always found in ethical frameworks or policy documents regulating the safety of AI technologies.[15] The jargon-heavy language used by experts may also alienate community members and prevent legitimate public endorsement of AI technologies from being sourced.[16] The removal of AI ethics from the fertile grounds of everyday public discourse sows the seed for community distrust targeted at key decision-makers in various proximities to power-holding authorities, especially when the public has been negatively affected by historical episodes of top-down enforced change.

The current landscape of AI ethical frameworks shows a high degree of converging values and principles (e.g. transparency, fairness, responsibility, and trust).[17] However, this homogeneity should not be taken as a sign that existing guidelines or documents have achieved widespread consensus or received genuine endorsements from communities across the globe. With international discourse on AI ethics dominated by wealthier nations, there remain unequal levels of participation from under-representation geographies such as Africa,

---

[15]   Thilo Hagendorff, 'The Ethics of AI Ethics: An Evaluation of Guidelines' (2020) 30 *Minds and Machines* 99. See also Jess Whittlestone and others, 'The Role and Limits of Principles in AI Ethics: Towards a Focus on Tensions', *Proceedings of the 2019 AAAI/ACM Conference on AI, Ethics, and Society* (Association for Computing Machinery 2019) https://doi.org/10.1145/3306618.3314289 accessed 24 May 2022.

[16]   Lindsey Conklin and others, 'Communicating About the Social Implications of AI: A FrameWorks Strategic Brief' (FrameWorks Institute) https://www.frameworksinstitute.org/publication/communicating-about-the-social-implications-of-ai-a-frameworks-strategic-brief/ accessed 5 September 2022.

[17]   Yi Zeng, Enmeng Lu and Cunqing Huangfu, 'Linking Artificial Intelligence Principles' [2018] arXiv:1812.04814 [cs] http://arxiv.org/abs/1812.04814 accessed 7 January 2022.

South and Central America, and Central Asia. The result is the absence of local knowledge and cultural pluralism in the official documents used to regulate AI technologies.[18]

In the dominant Silicon Valley-style iterations of AI ethics, the overarching spirit of instrumental reasoning has been left undisturbed and unquestioned. As novel technological inventions, AI technologies are seen as a neutral means to an end.[19] Yet, the ambition to dominate markets by appropriating human labour and natural resources forces AI innovation into serving the neoliberal market agenda of wealth creation.[20] By association, AI ethical frameworks undertaken by private enterprises become a self-regulatory exercise to dissuade 'hard law' or legally binding regulatory actions. When cast in this light, it becomes clear that ethical principles and values in corporate governance documents were never intended to represent or advocate for the collective interests of data subjects impacted by the activities of the wider AI ecosystem.

The rhetoric that technological enterprises based in Silicon Valley (or the organizations replicating their models in other geographical locations) use to advocate for the ethicalness of AI systems, as has been revealed above, can be unpacked based on its fundamental philosophical underpinnings. In 'Irreducibly Social Good',[21] Charles Taylor summarizes the prevalent ideologies embedded into modern societies to the extent that they have become a default part of everyday life:

- *Consequentialism* – arriving at value judgements of 'good' or 'bad' by weighing outcomes and states of affairs instead of the intrinsic moral quality of actions based on other 'metaphysical winnowing' that cannot be measured in instrumental terms.
- *Utilitarianism* – assessing states of affairs based on how much happiness or satisfaction they give to human agents. The utility of scenarios generally refers to what people find satisfying, enjoyable or generally positive.
- *Atomism* – the utilities to be weighed in states of affairs are those of *individuals*.

---

[18]   Anna Jobin, Marcello Ienca and Effy Vayena, 'The Global Landscape of AI Ethics Guidelines' (2019) 1 *Nature Machine Intelligence* 389, https://doi.org/10.1038/s42256-019-0088-2 accessed 20 April 2023.

[19]   Don Ihde *Technics and Praxis*. Boston Studies in the Philosophy of Science, 24. (Dordrecht: Springer Netherlands, 2019), doi:10.1007/978-94-009-9900-8 accessed 20 April 2023, pp.40–50, 66–81.

[20]   See chapter 6 of Mark Findlay, *Globalisation, Populism, Pandemics and the Law: The Anarchy and the Ecstasy.* (Cheltenham: Edward Elgar, 2021).

[21]   Charles Taylor, *Philosophical Arguments* (Harvard University Press 1995).

The third point seems self-evident in the context of the 21st century, where the living and working conditions have encouraged individualized notions of self-identities. But the significant implications of the 'atomist' ethic should be underestimated, given how this method of pursuing social good is motivated by instrumental and individualized standards:

> All wholes have to be understood in terms of the parts that compose them – but societies are made up of individuals. The events and states which are the subjects of study in society are ultimately made of the events and states of component individuals. In the end, only individuals choose and act. To think that society consists of something else, over and above these individual choices and actions, is to invoke some strange, mystical entity, a ghostly spirit of the collectivity, which no sober or respectable science can have any truck with.[22]

In this critical view of communitarian ethics, the social good deemed worthy of pursuit is determined by states of affairs that bring the most satisfaction to the greatest number of *individual people*. What vanishes from sight is the collective dimension that informs and shapes the values, preferences, and goals of individuals belonging to a shared community. To disavow the mystical presence of social collectivities, the atomist ethic collapses the notion of social good and objects of value into subjective feelings. What is lost in translation is a grounded appreciation of the histories of social ties connecting people to people from one generation to the next.[23] Where previous generations, especially in Asian societies, have prioritized the greater needs of their communities over and above their desires, this exhibition of pious self-sacrifice has been re-defined as a token of unacceptable oppression that forces individuals 'into a homogenous mold that is untrue to them'.[24] The forsaking of individual obligations to care for the well-being of the wider community membership, Taylor argues, is symptomatic of the problematic conversion of social issues, where 'the fate of peoples and cultures hangs in the balance', into the narrow confines of the individual's private pleasures, desires, and aversions directed at external circumstances.[25]

The rise of AI technologies in the wake of the Information Age has induced drastic changes in the basic conditions of modern living that far exceed the consequentialist, utilitarian, and atomized methods of measurement. With the application of efficient algorithms across many sectors, the labour markets,

---

[22] Ibid., pp.129–130.
[23] Ibid., p.130.
[24] Charles Taylor, 'The Politics of Recognition' in Amy Gutmann (ed), *Multiculturalism* (REV-Revised, Princeton University Press 1994) 43 http://www.jstor.org/stable/j.ctt7snkj.6 accessed 23 August 2021.
[25] Taylor, (n 21), p.141.

social communities, and even how people engage with their finances, education, and healthcare have all been transformed.[26] These changes in the conditions of now AI-employing institutions and their states of affairs belong to a causal chain of events reaching far back into pre-AI histories, which are not reduceable to the actions and responsibilities performed by individuals existing today.[27] Furthermore, defining the societal impacts of technological changes with a ruler determined by subjectivist and individualized terms neglects critical aspects of society that do not concern any specific and singular person: rules, offices, statuses, laws, and customs that govern appropriate behaviours in social relationships.[28] These issues pose a challenge to AI ethics discourse, as the inadequacy of ethical subjectivism in addressing the collective fates of vulnerable data subjects reveals a far more diluted and murkier sense of ethical responsibility: is there a collective and shared duty in the AI ecosystem to govern responsible and safe AI innovation for community benefit?

Faced with overly abstract and idealistic ethical principles, AI practitioners in technology companies are left wondering how they can begin to redress the downstream effects of their creation, given the limited scope and resources available to their spheres of influence.[29] In broader law-and-policy-making efforts to regulate AI safety, there is often limited to no room for negotiating how humans and machines ought to exist in a shared world (and what implications this may hold for the wider design choices applied to AI technologies). Indeed, mainstream formulations of AI ethics assumes the belief that 'AI is here to stay', and ethical principles are used to brand or validate product efficacy. Guarantees concerning the technological safety of AI systems end up overshadowing the element of choice from the data-subjects needed to achieve legitimate community acceptance – going above and beyond public passivity – of such technologies.[30] If one accepts the observation that AI roll-out is a *non-neutral* process that impacts people, society and the environment, the task of AI ethics is clarified: it is a regulatory instrument that helps key deci-

---

[26] Jacques Bughin and others, 'Artificial Intelligence: The Next Digital Frontier?' https://apo.org.au/node/210501 accessed 25 May 2022.

[27] Taylor (n 21), pp.129–130.

[28] Morten Bay, 'Four Challenges to Confucian Virtue Ethics in Technology' (2021) 19 *Journal of Information, Communication and Ethics in Society* 358.

[29] Michael A Madaio and others, 'Co-Designing Checklists to Understand Organizational Challenges and Opportunities around Fairness in AI' [2020] Proceedings of the 2020 CHI Conference on Human Factors in Computing Systems 1.

[30] Alicia Wee and Mark Findlay, 'AI and Data Use: Surveillance Technology and Community Disquiet in the Age of COVID-19' (Social Science Research Network 2020) SSRN Scholarly Paper ID 3715993 https://papers.ssrn.com/abstract=3715993 accessed 2 December 2020.

sion parties consider anticipated areas of impact alongside ways to provoke changes to achieve desired outcomes.

In its current form, AI ethics is armed with principles, values, and certificates, which are generally slow at responding to prevailing externalities underpinning the development and widespread adoption of AI technologies. Contrary to the utopian promise of using technological innovation to disrupt the status quo, Jobin et al.'s (2019) work reveals the ill-balanced landscape of the international discourse on AI ethics and the associated risks of AI technologies further entrenching long histories of the unequal power dynamic between the 'rich/poor' and 'developed/developing' communities.[31] Lacking contributions from under-represented regions and communities, the narrow construct of the AI governance agenda points to the subjugation or expulsion of other modes of thinking that do not conform to the dominant perspectives of North America, Europe, and other wealthy nations from Asia and the Middle East. With 'AI for social good' used as a convenient tagline without genuine desires for positive change towards more equitable outcomes, the capture of AI ethics by technological hegemonies represents another dimension of the neo-colonial advancement from North to South worlds.[32]

The disruptive characteristics of AI ethics only enter the picture when key decision parties in the AI ecosystem can effectively counter ongoing ethics-washing initiatives, where ethical principles are used as convenient sources of positive corporate branding.[33] Widening access and participation in formulating AI ethics, which is essential to a more inclusive regulatory frame, does not simply seek to increase the absolute quantity of ethical perspectives. Concrete and meaningful integration of diverse ethical orientations seen in

---

[31]   Meredith Whittaker, 'The Steep Cost of Capture' (2021) 28 *Interactions* (New York, N.Y.) 50; Jobin er al., (n 18).

[32]   Shakir Mohamed, Marie-Therese Png and William Isaac, 'Decolonial AI: Decolonial Theory as Sociotechnical Foresight in Artificial Intelligence' (2020) 33 *Philosophy & Technology* 659; Heather Widdows, 'Is Global Ethics Moral Neo-Colonialism? An Investigation of the Issue in the Context of Bioethics' (2007) 21 *Bioethics* 305; Karen Hao, 'Artificial Intelligence Is Creating a New Colonial World Order' [2022] *MIT Technology Review* https://www.technologyreview.com/ 2022/04/19/1049592/artificial-intelligence-colonialism/ accessed 20 April 2022. See also Ricardo Vinuesa and others, 'The Role of Artificial Intelligence in Achieving the Sustainable Development Goals' (2020) 11 *Nature Communications* 233. and L M Ong and M Findlay (To be published). A Realist's Account of AI for SDGs: Power, Inequality and AI in Community. In L Floridi and F Mazzi (eds), *The Ethics of Artificial Intelligence for the Sustainable Development Goals* (Springer Nature, 2023).

[33]   Karen Yeung, Andrew Howes and Ganna Pogrebna, 'AI Governance by Human Rights-Centred Design, Deliberation and Oversight: An End to Ethics Washing' in *The Oxford Handbook of AI Ethics* (Oxford University Press, 2019) https://papers.ssrn.com/ abstract=3435011 accessed 12 July 2020.

communities across the globe demands, first and foremost, the demotion of AI technologies' primary purpose as a wealth creation tool. Without this commitment, any insights sourced from diverse systems of thought across many contemplative paradigms (e.g., religious, spiritual, or philosophical intellectual lineages) are likely to be deemed irrelevant to the neoliberal and capitalistic motivations underpinning AI roll-out. Inviting greater engagements with a diverse range of humanistic values in pluralistic communities triggers radical disruption necessary for revitalising AI ethics as an *active* practice. Unless ethics becomes critical and self-reflexive of its operational contexts, there is a looming danger of pushing global communities towards an increasingly narrow trajectory of techno-solutionism.[34] What should not vanish from sight is the collective voice that ought to scrutinize AI innovation beyond the dictates of commercial interests and political expediency in order to decide whether it is necessary or desirable to integrate AI into community spaces.[35]

Reforming AI ethics as a regulatory instrument attuned to community contexts has its challenges. Methods of sourcing inputs from data-subjects and community members to determine the acceptable roles and purposes served by AI technologies are sometimes unquantifiable and hard to measure or scale up. An example is applying social imagination to identify the types of AI futures worth aspiring towards and others deemed undesirable.[36] This method of representation and inclusion can help create more room in AI ethics to accommodate grassroots negotiation of AI futures unfolding across diverse localities; however, it remains to be seen whether existing governance styles and mechanisms are genuinely receptive to prioritizing community sentiments of AI's integration into their everyday lives. Indeed, the level of public discussion envisioned depends on having appropriate participatory pathways to enable different demographics of society to contribute towards AI ethics formulations firmly rooted in their local or regional contexts.[37] Practical hurdles exist between transitioning smaller conversations that have historically taken

---

[34] Elma Hajric, 'A Commentary on Covid-19 Contact-Tracing Apps and Broader Societal Implications of Technosolutionism', *2020 IEEE International Symposium on Technology and Society (ISTAS)* (2020).

[35] Elisabetta Ferrari, 'Technocracy Meets Populism: The Dominant Technological Imaginary of Silicon Valley' (2020) 13 *Communication, Culture and Critique* 121.

[36] Sarah Copeland and Aldo de Moor, 'Community Digital Storytelling for Collective Intelligence: Towards a Storytelling Cycle of Trust' (2018) 33 *AI & Society* 101; Phil Macnaghten, 'Towards an Anticipatory Public Engagement Methodology: Deliberative Experiments in the Assembly of Possible Worlds Using Focus Groups' (2021) 21 *Qualitative Research* 3.

[37] Elizabeth Bondi and others, 'Envisioning Communities: A Participatory Approach Towards AI for Social Good' [2021] Proceedings of the 2021 AAAI/ACM Conference on AI, Ethics, and Society 425.

place in local neighbourhoods into large-scale models of online dialogues or international public forums.[38] Nevertheless, without these critical pathways to ground AI ethics in community contexts, there looms the risk of wholesale transplantations of Western or Euro-centric values into marginalized communities embodying different norms, standards and values.[39]

Accepting the challenges described above, it remains true that embracing ethical pluralism is foundational to community-centric AI ethical formulations. The ultimate goal of integrating historically under-represented perspectives into AI governance – though there is likely to be more than one 'goal' – is not to produce an all-encompassing framework. Even if this is not the explicit intention, this one-size-fits-all approach risks banalizing or homogenizing the distinctive moral, ethical, intellectual, and cultural lineages from non-Western parts of the world in favour of dominant iterations of AI ethical frameworks.[40] Rather, it is necessary to surrender the false view that ethics, as an ongoing phenomenon lived out by diverse people across varied geographies, can be captured meaningfully by decontextualized and universalist principles. Community-centric AI ethics only disrupts the status quo by positioning 'people' over 'profits' and inviting diverse communities to negotiate the ideal AI futures suited to their local contexts.

Finally, the scope of AI ethics as a regulatory instrument to provoke change and achieve desired outcomes remains intimately connected with the conditions of interpersonal trust in the community. Given the need for cooperation among key players of the regional and global AI ecosystems, AI decision-making frameworks retain effectiveness through close coordination to establish a cohesive regulatory approach that minimizes AI risks and harm.[41] Even when striving for a diversity of thought, the willingness to bridge anticipated cultural or regulatory differences – not seeing localized variations of AI regulatory solutions as barriers – requires the spirit of solidarity and togetherness to motivate key stakeholders to pursue common goals and shared interests.[42] With this in mind, the next section will demonstrate how community-centric AI ethics can restore previously strained trust relations among people and communities.

---

[38] Peter Muhlberger, Jennifer Stromer-Galley and Nick Webb, 'Public Policy and Obstacles to the Virtual Agora: Insights from the Deliberative e-Rulemaking Project' (2011) 16 *Information Polity* 197.

[39] Arunoday Saha, 'Technological Innovation and Western Values' (1998) 20 *Technology in Society* 499.

[40] Widdows, (n 32).

[41] Seán S ÓhÉigeartaigh and others, 'Overcoming Barriers to Cross-Cultural Cooperation in AI Ethics and Governance' (2020) 33 *Philosophy & Technology* 571.

[42] Mohamed et al., (n 32).

1.2   Rebuilding Trust via a Community-centric Ethical Decision-making Framework

To recap, community-centric AI is motivated by the understanding that align-ing AI design and deployment choices with the host community's norms or standards will improve public acceptance and trust of AI technologies. The conscientious integration of AI technologies in selective areas of community spaces depends on the level of communication, coordination, and willingness among the key decision parties to ensure AI capabilities are directed to meet the needs and goals of members in the host community.

In the analysis so far, the working definition of 'community' bears some explanation. Although often intertwined with the concept of 'society', the idea of community is more flexible in its reference to 'a diversity of social collec-tivities, commitments and systems of interests, values or beliefs, coexisting, overlapping and interpenetrating'.[43] It can, but need not, take shape in tradi-tional formations: a community of people can refer to a nation-state or even smaller groupings of people who coexist in a shared environment in a defined geographical space (e.g., a local neighbourhood). What binds a community of people together, according to Roger Cotterrell, is the social relationships that require mutual interpersonal trust to thrive and flourish. This definition of community has a quality of stretchiness (or 'stickiness') that encompasses people living across geographies connected through a shared sense of belong-ing and mutual concern for their community members.[44] The spirit of solidar-ity that ensures the longevity of a living community does not apply only to *physical* communities marked out with external borders. People living through convergent social realities can also form communities based on similar inter-ests, beliefs, values or other sources of affinities that encourage the formation of social ties and interpersonal trust. Although the notion of community has never been fixed, enclosed or static, some have argued that this shared sense of collective identity is built on friends-and-foe hostile relations: 'The insiders in a we-group are in a relation of peace, order, law, government and industry to each other. Their relation to all outsiders, or other groups, is one of war and plunder, except so far as agreements have modified it.'[45]

---

[43]   Roger Cotterrell, *Law, Culture and Society: Legal Ideas in the Mirror of Social Theory* (1st edn, Routledge, 2006). https://doi.org/10.4324/9781351217989 accessed 20 April 2023.

[44]   Roger Cotterrell, 'Law, Emotion and Affective Community' (Social Science Research Network 2018) SSRN Scholarly Paper ID 3212860 https://papers.ssrn.com/abstract=3212860 accessed 3 December 2020.

[45]   Hoggs and Abrams, 1988 cited in Cotterrell, (n 43), p.71.

Since the realities of community arrangements often escape this oversimplified binary, it is crucial to highlight that negative and hostile attitudes to outsiders need not preoccupy the formation of healthy community identities. Communal groups can gather around shared causes of mutual support driven by a:

> *shared sense of collective experience or destiny*, which does not have to emphasise a distinction from outsiders, nor indeed focus on relations with outsiders … though it may attach special importance to resources of mutual support between members and the need to protect these (if necessary against 'outside' interference).[46]

An example of a unifying frame of shared fates is the rapid changes in climate ecologies and natural environments, which the United Nations has called the 'defining crisis of our time'.[47] The double-edged nature of AI innovation in addressing *and* compounding this global challenge is evidenced by mixed environmental consequences.[48] High carbon footprint levels stemming from the increasing use of AI and big data analytics,[49] which presents ecological challenges,[50] could also bring innovation to efficient management of energy supply chains that enable sustainable living.[51] Given the widespread impacts of human activity on climate and ecosystems, the critical dual role of AI technologies to induce positive and negative disruptions brings into focus the presence of collective destiny in responsible governance of AI capabilities for community benefit.[52]

Even so, the bounds of the community contain tensions within itself that could undermine the immediacy of the shared sense of collective experience. A pertinent example is the common threat of the COVID-19 virus, wherein diverse communities can encounter drastically different tracks of reality during the global pandemic. In the implementation of COVID-19 containment strat-

---

[46]   Cotterrell, (n 43), p.72. Emphasis mine.

[47]   'The Climate Crisis – A Race We Can Win' (*United Nations*) https://www.un .org/en/un75/climate-crisis-race-we-can-win accessed 26 September 2022.

[48]   Benedetta Brevini, 'Black Boxes, Not Green: Mythologizing Artificial Intelligence and Omitting the Environment' (2020) 7 *Big Data & Society* https://doi .org/10.1177/205395172093 accessed 20 April 2023.

[49]   Payal Dhar, 'The Carbon Impact of Artificial Intelligence' (2020) 2 *Nature Machine Intelligence* 423.

[50]   Josh Cowls and others, 'The AI Gambit: Leveraging Artificial Intelligence to Combat Climate Change—Opportunities, Challenges, and Recommendations' (2021) AI & Society https://doi.org/10.1007/s00146-021-01294-x accessed 11 February 2022.

[51]   Rajan Jose and others, 'Artificial Intelligence-Driven Circular Economy as a Key Enabler for Sustainable Energy Management' (2020) 2 *Materials Circular Economy* 8.

[52]   Kyle Whyte, 'Too Late for Indigenous Climate Justice: Ecological and Relational Tipping Points' (2020) 11 *WIREs Climate Change* e603.

egies across the world, excessive vaccination hoarding by wealthier nations has left others without direct access to vital medical provisions,[53] leading to broken trust and entrenched global economic-and-power relations that vaccine diplomacy cannot undo or negate.[54] This setback in international cooperation also highlights the need for a cohesive and collaborative approach to tackle large-scale problems affecting the global community in honour of the fundamental interconnectedness of human beings co-habiting in a shared world.

Adopting the lens of shared fates – albeit with fierce disputes at the margins – this chapter proposes an alternative mode of ethical decision-making to rebuild interpersonal and institutional trust. It may seem counter-intuitive to suggest public trust as an essential factor or a social force regulating the collective determination of AI's intended utility in the host community. After all, research efforts into the recipe for 'trustworthy AI' reveal the implicit assumption that public trust will emerge as a natural outcome of the objective qualities of AI systems.[55] It is widely agreed that the functionality and performance of AI systems play a significant role in determining human trust attitudes.[56] Yet, other human and environmental factors also influence trust formation. Where human trustors place inappropriate levels of trust in trustees,[57] situations of over-trusting or under-trusting autonomous vehicles independent of their functional reliability reveal the subjective psychological dimensions of trust choices and behaviours.[58] It follows that improving the technical attributes of AI systems is a *necessary* but *insufficient* way of building a foundation of shared trust leading to community acceptance of such technologies. Discussions of trust and its preconditions, in effect, shift the focus out of laboratory settings into the ever-changing dynamics of community contexts that

---

[53] Niladri Chatterjee, Zaad Mahmood and Eleonor Marcussen, 'Politics of Vaccine Nationalism in India: Global and Domestic Implications' (2021) 48 *Forum for Development Studies* 357.

[54] John Harrington and David Ngira, 'Vaccine Diplomacy and the Agency of African States: What Can We Learn from Kenya?' https://hal.archives-ouvertes.fr/hal-03537537 accessed 11 February 2022.

[55] Ben Shneiderman, 'Human-Centered Artificial Intelligence: Reliable, Safe & Trustworthy' (2020) 36 *International Journal of Human-Computer Interaction* 495.

[56] Peter A Hancock and others, 'A Meta-Analysis of Factors Affecting Trust in Human-Robot Interaction' (2011) 53 *Human Factors* 517.

[57] Mariarosaria Taddeo, 'On The Risks of Trusting Artificial Intelligence: The Case of Cybersecurity' (2020) *SSRN Electronic Journal* https://www.ssrn.com/abstract=3730651 accessed 23 February 2021.

[58] Kai Holländer, Philipp Wintersberger and Andreas Butz, 'Overtrust in External Cues of Automated Vehicles: An Experimental Investigation', *Proceedings of the 11th International Conference on Automotive User Interfaces and Interactive Vehicular Applications* (ACM 2019) https://dl.acm.org/doi/10.1145/3342197.3344528 accessed 27 September 2022.

complicate the allegedly straightforward path toward public trust. In shaping community-centric AI ethics as a regulatory instrument, shared trust is built when ethical decision-making processes can prioritize the voices of vulnerable data subjects to formulate the acceptable boundaries within which AI technologies should operate.[59]

Contrary to disengaged models of AI governance that neglect sentiments of public distrust towards AI technologies, the proposed alternative framework seeks to integrate community voices into AI design and deployment choices. If the intended purpose of calibrating trust levels towards AI technologies is not to eliminate voices of dissent, the application of community-centric AI ethics can help to activate and strengthen existing social ties. Unlike policy-making scenarios of public passivity where AI actors' thinking goes unchallenged, this alternative model embraces disagreements as a key feature of healthy social communities working through natural processes of negotiating, updating, and reforming its norms and standards.[60] As such, the desired regulatory response is not to reconcile value differences by erasing or downplaying localized variations of ethical perspectives. Instead, leveraging participatory mechanisms that can build consensus within and across pluralistic communities is key.[61] By identifying the key stakeholders involved in AI governance, the ethical responsibilities become distributed across the decision pipeline; collaborative and joined efforts in steering decisions about AI design, creation, and deployment are characterized by active partnerships in the community. It follows that establishing healthy interpersonal trust relations is *necessarily prior* to building AI-human trust.[62]

Prioritizing consensus-building with data-subjects and community members can also improve interpersonal trust on a global level. Research has shown the potential of inviting public participation into global governance spheres to complement existing local and regional initiatives.[63] To recap, community-centric

---

[59] Mona Sloane, 'To Make AI Fair, Here's What We Must Learn to Do' (2022) 605 *Nature* 9.

[60] Nicolas Berberich, Toyoaki Nishida and Shoko Suzuki, 'Harmonizing Artificial Intelligence for Social Good' (2020) 33 *Philosophy & Technology* 613.

[61] Iason Gabriel, 'Artificial Intelligence, Values, and Alignment' (2020) 30 *Minds and Machines* 411.

[62] Sonja Zmerli, Kenneth Newton and José Ramón Montero, 'Trust in People, Confidence in Political Institutions, and Satisfaction with Democracy' in Jan W Van Deth, José Ramón Montero and Anders Westholm (eds), *Citizenship and Involvement in European Democracies: A Comparative Analysis* (Taylor & Francis Group 2006) http://ebookcentral.proquest.com/lib/smu/detail.action?docID=292968 accessed 26 April 2021.

[63] Bondi and others, (n 37); Eduardo Belinchon and others, 'Towards an Inclusive Future in AI. A Global Participatory Process' (Social Science Research Network 2019)

AI ethics seeks to enable public participation in deliberating the social and legal responsibilities of AI. Realistically, this aspiration requires a wider global initiative to raise digital literacy and resist current trends of unequal participation, where voices of the Global South have been largely missing from AI governance discourse.[64] Pressing issues should also be communicated in jargon-free language and accessible formats.[65] It is also vital to ensure that elected government representatives can demonstrate a workable and sufficient understanding of the public's concerns regarding AI technologies.[66] Data-subjects who may lack technical knowledge of trending buzzwords (such as big data, machine learning, neural networks, and algorithms) rely on the advocacy of elected representatives and law-and-policymakers to hold accountable powerful companies. As such, the cultivation of techno-moral wisdom for all members of the global community will enable more robust negotiations of the required governance mechanisms to protect human well-being and preserve the fragility of shared trust amidst rapid technological change.[67]

The proposed alternative of community-centric AI ethics requires more radical changes than minor tweaks to mainstream ethical frameworks that have arisen mainly from the Western-European intellectual lineages. Even granting the assumption that the principles of harm prevention and international human rights are universally acceptable in AI governance, the concrete application of these values requires further dialogue and grounding within other worldviews and systems of beliefs.[68] Inviting greater diversity of thought – featuring local voices, local knowledge, and local communities – is essential to realign AI innovation trajectories with communally-located aspirations. By diversifying sources of knowledge used to regulate AI technologies, the appreciation of ethical pluralism holds the potential to revive the conviction that people

---

SSRN Scholarly Paper 3505425 https://papers.ssrn.com/abstract=3505425 accessed 25 May 2022.

[64]   Anne Gerdes, 'An Inclusive Ethical Design Perspective for a Flourishing Future with Artificial Intelligent Systems' (2018) 9 *European Journal of Risk Regulation : EJRR* 677.

[65]   Atoosa Kasirzadeh, 'Reasons, Values, Stakeholders: A Philosophical Framework for Explainable Artificial Intelligence' (arXiv 2021) arXiv:2103.00752 http://arxiv.org/abs/2103.00752 accessed 25 May 2022.

[66]   Eva Erman and Markus Furendal, 'The Global Governance of Artificial Intelligence: Some Normative Concerns' (2022) *Moral Philosophy and Politics* https://www.degruyter.com/document/doi/10.1515/mopp-2020-0046/html accessed 25 May 2022.

[67]   Gerdes, (n 64); Shannon Vallor, 'Moral Deskilling and Upskilling in a New Machine Age: Reflections on the Ambiguous Future of Character' (2015) 28 *Philosophy & Technology* 107.

[68]   Hagendorff, (n 15).

can and should come together to tackle shared risks, threats, and challenges. Phrased differently, the deliberate turn towards a 'deeper collective truth of our interconnectedness' ensures that community-centric AI ethics do not collapse into the realm of *subjectivism*,[69] where the call to action for tackling common causes must confront individualistic judgements of personal morality.

Given the task, it may be too severe to promote the wholesale rejection of existing principle-based AI ethics. Recognizing the usefulness of ethical principles such as fairness and transparency does not preclude adopting a more culturally nuanced and reflexive approach in shifting theory into practice.[70] The mistake of AI ethics is assuming that a one-size-fits-all to regulating AI technologies is even viable.[71] Doing so risks further disengagement with community contexts or depersonalization due to negligent universal frameworks papering over divergent realities. Returning to the theme of building trust, it would be naïve to assume there is a standard or fixed formula for applying ethics to guarantee improved public trust judgements concerning AI technologies. Since there is no easy answer to the complex challenges of AI regulation, striving for more robust public participation is one of many options to enable a community-centric regulatory approach seeking to build shared trust and achieve broader public acceptance of AI technologies.

When integrating community voices to interpret and translate the mantra of "AI for social good" into concrete regulatory measures,[72] the goal is using consensus-building to negotiate between realistic and aspirational forms of governance. The main reason for pushing against existing boundaries of what is acceptable or otherwise is revealed in the imperfect nature of human societies. Put differently, without a long-term conviction to overcome existing flaws in heuristic thinking (whether individually or collectively manifested), the trajectory of AI innovation will inevitably get caught up in the messy entanglements of conventional human biases, false opinions, and contradictions.[73] To overcome this limiting factor, the task of debugging AI of biases and discrimination requires human actors to seek technical solutions that avoid the direct transfer of ethical and moral blind spots from data samples into the

---

[69] 'John Prendergast on Non-Dual Awareness and Wisdom for the 21st Century' https://futureoflife.org/2021/02/09/john-prendergast-on-non-dual-awareness-and-wisdom-for-the-21st-century/ accessed 19 April 2021.

[70] Brent Mittelstadt, 'Principles Alone Cannot Guarantee Ethical AI' (2019) 1 *Nature Machine Intelligence* 501.

[71] Gabriel, (n 61), pp.424–425.

[72] 'Artificial Intelligence for Social Good' (Association of Pacific Rim Universities (APRU) 2020) https://apru.org/resource/artificial-intelligence-for-social-good/ accessed 9 April 2021.

[73] Hagendorff, (n 15).

inferences made by increasingly powerful AI systems. Therefore, it is critical for key actors in the AI ecosystem – including the public – to cultivate their shared abilities to update beliefs, values, and identity.[74] Doing so would also strengthen social ties and build shared trust in the community, corresponding to what is true and good for all humanity.

By appreciating the ethical priorities of diverse communities across the globe, a far more vibrant and holistic understanding of what AI-human trust relations can or ought to be is presented. Embedded within community-centric AI ethics is the conviction to leverage community voices to determine whether a stronger presence of AI technologies is even a desirable goal worth pursuing. The 'disruptive' side of AI ethics, as a regulatory instrument to rebuild shared trust, pushes AI actors to make decisions with community benefits in mind. Therein lies the potential to disrupt the status quo, redistribute decision-making power and extend ethical responsibilities *horizontally* across the AI ecosystem.[75]

2. EMOTIONS

So far, this analysis has established the basis for AI ethics to operate as an ethical decision-making framework to rebuild shared trust. What requires further examination is the causal influences of trust as a human psychological phenomenon mediated by human emotions.[76] Prior research on human-robot interactions reveals affective influences that restrict the effectiveness of ethical principles alone in convincing public trust.[77] To retain regulatory relevance, AI

---

[74] Ibid. Although this view interweaves ethical progress with personal/collective emotional adjustments, Peter Railton offers a similar insight of using evidence and well-reasoned argument to debug human biases and make continual improvements on one's beliefs about the world (see 'Peter Railton on Moral Learning and Metaethics in AI Systems' https://futureoflife.org/2020/08/18/peter-railton-on-moral-learning-and-metaethics-in-ai-systems/ accessed 17 December 2020). This position connects with the work of John Dewey, *Human Nature and Conduct: An Introduction to Social Psychology* (New York: Random House, 1922) on how epistemological enquiries – what we can know about the world and what we can know about ourselves as *feeling/thinking* beings – are moral enquiries. Rationality and emotions are two sides of the same coin which constitute a complex picture of human morality.

[75] Josephine Seah and Mark James Findlay, 'Communicating Ethics across the AI Ecosystem' (2021) *SSRN Electronic Journal* https://www.ssrn.com/abstract=3895522 accessed 2 August 2021.

[76] Simone Belli and Fernando Broncano, 'Trust as a Meta-Emotion' (2017) 48 *Metaphilosophy* 430.

[77] Wenxi Zhang, Willow Wong and Mark Findlay, 'Trust in Robotics: A Multi-Staged Decision-Making Approach to Robots in Community' (2023) *AI & Soc.* https://doi.org/10.1007/s00146-023-01705-1 accessed 25 June 2023.

actors involved in implementing ethical frameworks must also monitor social conditions that trigger divisive emotions and erode shared trust in the community. When AI innovation advances wider social causes that unite people (e.g., sustainability, peace, justice), the decision-makers are better positioned to convince public acceptance for the legitimate purposes of AI roll-out into community spaces.

2.1   Emotions, Perception and Judgements

Mainstream iterations of AI ethics operate on the core assumption that human recipients of AI technologies behave only as rational agents,[78] who are most convinced by the official government documents or safety certifications that guarantee AI 'trustworthiness'.[79] However, the jargon-heavy terminologies of AI have been glamourized to obscure accurate public understanding of AI capabilities and their potential impact on society.[80] Due to information asymmetries, the alienation of data-subject risks compounding public perception that the knowledge advancement of AI innovation is elitist,[81] or that law-and-policymaking endeavours have generally been disengaged from the concerns and interests of the everyday person.[82] As such, the *knowledge gaps* between AI actors and the data subjects risk engendering *trust gaps.*

Associated with the technical requirements of AI's robustness is the challenge of maintaining critical public engagement against habitual or blind trust in the decision-makers.[83] In the absence of relevant expertise or knowledge to engage with governance discourse, the average user draws from communal sentiments to determine whether they should trust something or someone in their initial encounters; yet, the trust which has been extended can also be revoked due to newly-occurred suspicions or reservations *separate* from the initial encounter in question. In the context of AI roll-out, people may be overly trusting of AI technologies introduced and deployed by familiar sources

---

[78]   Roger Brubaker, 'The Ethical Irrationality of the World', in *The Limits of Rationality* (Routledge 1984).

[79]   Rei Kurohi, 'S'pore to Invest $50m over 5 Years to Build Digital Trust' *The Straits Times* (Singapore, 15 July 2021) https://www.straitstimes.com/tech/spore-to -invest-50m-over-5-years-to-build-digital-trust accessed 13 August 2021.

[80]   Conklin and others, (n 16).

[81]   D Boulter, 'Public Perception of Science and Associated General Issues for the Scientist' (1999) 50 *Phytochemistry* 1.

[82]   Nick Vaughan-Williams and Daniel Stevens, 'Vernacular Theories of Everyday (in)Security: The Disruptive Potential of Non-Elite Knowledge' (2016) 47 *Security Dialogue* 40.

[83]   Adriano Fabris, 'Can We Trust Machines? The Role of Trust in Technological Environments' in Adriano Fabris (ed), *Trust* (Springer International Publishing 2020).

with pre-existing histories of (dis)trust and (dis)belief. Conversely, individuals or social collectives gripped by fear or anxieties may reject AI systems that have undergone robust scrutiny and are certified to be safe (and thus, allegedly, 'trustworthy' by default). When people draw on their evolving *personal* understanding of what *feels* dangerous, foreign, or intrusive, the causal influences underpinning the human choice of trust and mistrust trace back to the inextricable origins of past experiences. The instinctive and habitual dimensions of trust reveal the value-laden processes of human decision-making, where the social influences of affectivity challenge the strict hold of scientific rationality.

Where affectivity reveals the human susceptibility to hold unwarranted beliefs, the diminished role of rationality in steering ethical decision-making should cause alarm to AI practitioners and decision-makers. If people arrive at their decisions to trust or distrust a new piece of technology *somewhat* independently from the technical specificities of AI systems, there is a compelling reason for decision parties to adopt regulatory approaches that can monitor and address the externalities holding sway over positive, mixed, or negative community reactions. In this case, theoretical and empirical mapping of transformative social changes or other causal motivators of trust can yield regulatory insights that enable key actors to improve public sentiments towards AI technologies.[84]

On the other hand, if the default mode of AI regulation continues to be abstract universal frameworks that gloss over the social influences of human emotions, negative public perceptions of AI ethics as concerned with legal compliance would lead to apathy, indifference or helplessness directed towards the technocratic bureaucracy of AI governance. For community members who believe they lack the agency or the knowledge to influence change, the choice to engage in trust (or distrust) is reduced to a reluctant acceptance that AI roll-out is inevitable. This 'trust and forget' attitude encourages the *opposite* of meaningful public oversight, as the evolving challenges posed by AI systems will not be weighed up alongside potential benefits in an ongoing process of negotiation.[85]

Given the challenges presented above, AI safety is a necessary but insufficient condition to warrant community trust.[86] To optimize positive trust outcomes in recipient communities, AI actors are called to the social contexts

---

[84]   Brett W Israelsen and Nisar R Ahmed, '"Dave...I Can Assure You ...That It's Going to Be All Right ..." A Definition, Case for, and Survey of Algorithmic Assurances in Human-Autonomy Trust Relationships' (2019) 51 *ACM Computing Surveys* 1.

[85]   Taddeo, (n 57).

[86]   Bran Knowles and John T Richards, 'The Sanction of Authority: Promoting Public Trust in AI', *Proceedings of the 2021 ACM Conference on Fairness, Accountability,*

that shape community trust perceptions and judgements. Returning to an earlier point of analysis, efforts to dispel public fears based on false perceptions should also be made without manipulative techniques that undermine *genuine* reservations held by community members.[87] To summarize, critical engagement with trust-building requires key decision-makers to interpret the broader social contexts and cultural norms within which the notions of 'trust' or 'mistrust' take specific forms. The stronghold of popular wisdom over the general population also clarifies the need for AI regulatory approaches to consider practical ways of cultivating a more accurate public understanding of AI's risks and benefits. Addressing public sentiments of trust and distrust has been identified as essential to activating and maintaining shared trust across diverse community settings.

2.2   Emotions, Self/Community Identity and Trust

In addition to shaping public perceptions and trust judgements, human emotions also intensify social identities and community bonding. As per earlier analysis, emotions are deeply embedded into the ethical intuitions held by individuals and widely endorsed by the community. Assumptions of a 'common sense' approach to ethical decision-making are prevalent, even when community members support error-laden ethical norms and conventions. These personal and collective intuitions of what is right and wrong at times do not survive rational, scientific, or empirical interrogations.[88] Even so, culturally salient values reveal how people orientate their actions against those of other community members in their immediate environments. These inter-exchanges of ideas, values and shared meaning are simultaneously facilitated by and constitutive of the *affectivity* bound to a specific community. Yet, as a two-way causal interaction, this feedback loop can set in motion a double-edged force that holds the potential to solidify *and* destroy existing community bonding.

In *The Cultural Politics of Emotions*,[89] Sara Ahmed outlines the causal relationship between the circulation of human emotions within a social space and the formation of the *self-and-community* identity.[90] If human emotions are

---

and *Transparency* (Association for Computing Machinery 2021) https://doi.org/10 .1145/3442188.3445890 accessed 25 May 2022.

[87]   Rodrigo Ochigame, 'The Invention of "Ethical AI": How Big Tech Manipulates Academia to Avoid Regulation' (*The Intercept*, 21 December 2019) https://theintercept .com/2019/12/20/mit-ethical-ai-artificial-intelligence/ accessed 8 January 2021.

[88]   Peter Railton, 'Moral Learning: Conceptual Foundations and Normative Relevance' (2017) 167 *Cognition* 172.

[89]   Sara Ahmed, *The Cultural Politics of Emotion* (2nd edn, University Press 2014).

[90]   My own term, as italicized.

always inherently bound up with the entity – whether human, animate, or inanimate – that elicits the response out of the individual, what emerges is a vivid image of diverse affective economies mirroring the interweaving nature of living communities across the online and offline modes. Akin to how monetary values are assigned to commodities across different markets within a capitalist economy, feelings and emotions can also become 'stuck' to particular subjects, objects or spaces in levels of intensity or salience that fluctuate over time. This constitutes the 'affective economy', as Ahmed coined it, referring to emotions, values, and meaning that gain specific localized resonances across diverse cultures and communities.[91]

When affectivity is so tightly bound to community contexts, it is easy to assume that emotions are the culprits of entrenched divisions between nations. Yet, it would be inaccurate to point to affective-driven (dis)trust as the explanation for ongoing trade tensions in regional strategies toward AI ethics and governance. This conclusion is not a logical necessity, given the presence of *choice* in responding to any particularly salient emotion. Even when confronted with affective forces that intensify social bonding, each member still has the choice to participate, withdraw, or mitigate the affective influences operating in their immediate environment.[92] Localized variations in affective economies – correlating to each community's unique, implicit, and communally-grounded understanding of context-specific connections between values, meanings, and emotions – may not be the key perpetrator of community tension otherwise sourced from political or economic agendas.[93] Where the affective drive of social bonding is more pronounced, its operations would inevitably converge with other instrumental aims, such as the need for everyday coexistence and respectful conformity with the customs of a shared environment.[94] Since most communities depend on the goods and services pro-

---

[91] To avoid confusion, this analysis adopts the concept of 'affective economies' strictly outlined by Sara Ahmed. Although this term may be used elsewhere to describe the market incentive to manipulate consumer emotion, this chapter seeks not to engage with any suggestions of using AI as an instrumental tool to nudge consumer behaviours. This analysis refers only to Ahmed's articulation of 'affective economy' as describing the *laws in motion* which constitute the interrelatedness of external objects and subjects in the phenomenological world. As such, references to the 'affective economy' are used only to show the interoperative linkages between emotions, community values and decisions to trust/distrust.

[92] Amitai Etzioni, 'The Responsive Community: A Communitarian Perspective' (1996) 61 *American Sociological Review* 1.

[93] Vishali Sairam, Vincent S Heddesheimer and Joanna J Bryson, 'Economic Insecurity Increases Polarization and Decreases Trust' (SocArXiv, 11 July 2022) https://osf.io/preprints/socarxiv/cmfvb/ accessed 20 October 2022.

[94] Cotterrell, (n 43).

vided by other communities, the interlinked nature of AI ecosystems motivates the view that diversity on its own – or what John Rawls terms as 'reasonable pluralism' – need not be the originator or instigator of hostile conflicts.[95]

Nevertheless, the exercise of human choice in response to affective contestations will inform how social bonding occurs in the community. As Ronald de Sousa (2001) summarizes, '[E]motions are local to certain organisms in certain environments. Emotional repertoires can differ, as can the significance of their members, but these differences are not arbitrary. There is no independent access to the world revealed by emotion.'[96] When one's choice to participate as a community member is mediated by *reason* in the absence of coercion, manipulation, or other subliminal means of control, healthy social bonding occurs. However, when driven purely by intense emotions fuelled by false perceptions or ill will, these unhealthy social bonds can erode the conditions of shared trust and social cohesion.[97] As an example, without the force of affective-driven distrust to galvanize their *self-and-community* identities, supporters of far-right ideologies may not have activated new social bonds across online and offline environments with such unprecedented speed and strength.[98] Online culture of polarization reveals the dangers of social media platforms engendering cycles of emotional outrage that convince users to mistake 'sameness' of identity as the primary source of social solidarity.[99] Resulting from online communities

---

[95]   Gabriel, (n 61); Berberich, (n 60); Catherine Audard, *John Rawls* (Taylor & Francis Group 2006) http://ebookcentral.proquest.com/lib/smu/detail.action?docID= 1886904 accessed 31 March 2021.

[96]   Ronald de Sousa, 'Moral Emotions' (2001) 4 *Ethical Theory and Moral Practice* 109, 120.

[97]   This raises a fundamental question on whether it is possible to take a preventative measure over unhealthy social bonds to minimize negative consequences. There is no easy answer. Top-down control exercises to erase these social bonds fuelled by fear may stop the immediate spread of activities in these communities, such as in the case of social media platforms taking action to remove hateful online content. However, this does not address or resolve the underlying causes leading to the growth of these unhealthy social bonds in the community. Albeit highly aspirational, the practice of self-enquiry does hold *some* potential in resolving the *internal* factors exerting strain on existing social bonds; while the *external* causes may remain, individuals can still work on addressing their own biases to pave the way for healthier social bonds in service of what is collectively good for humanity.

[98]   Stephane J Baele, Lewys Brace and Travis G Coan, 'Uncovering the Far-Right Online Ecosystem: An Analytical Framework and Research Agenda' (2020) *Studies in Conflict & Terrorism* 1.

[99]   Saralyn Cruickshank, 'Moral Outrage Overload? How Social Media May Be Changing Our Brains' (*The Hub*, 25 September 2019) https://hub.jhu.edu/2019/09/25/molly-crockett-social-media-outrage/ accessed 11 February 2022.

built on hatred, insecurities, or fear of the 'other',[100] interpersonal trust constitutive of heterogenous communities in offline settings becomes eroded.

Due to the volatility of emotions, any external manipulation unmoderated by collective efforts to counter distrust can negatively impact the long-term social cohesion of diverse communities. Where the operations of AI technologies amplify hostile public sentiments across existing social fault lines, the use of emotional forces to instigate widespread communal disturbance then works against the overall viability of AI-human trust relations. Public disavowal of AI technologies becomes a mirror that reflects states of broken or strained social relationships in the community, where trust is no longer mutualized, available, or shared freely. The risks of online polarization rippling back into offline spaces require AI decision parties to take an institution-wide approach that safeguards community interests and rebuilds public trust.[101]

Accepting the looming question of which concrete mechanisms or processes are most suitable for meaningful community engagement, the starting point of resolving public fear and anxiety – especially if sourced from a place of vulnerability and prior victimization – should prioritize community voices. Identifying user needs and addressing ethical concerns across all stages of AI and data lifecycle requires community members to be positioned as co-creators who share the task of participatory design towards AI as a socially embedded tool. In this picture, AI actors and traditional institutions remain crucial in aligning AI roll-out with the host community's ethical norms and standards to rebuild public trust.[102]

2.3 Affectivity, Rationality, and Possible Responses from AI Ethics Sponsors

If the goal is applying community-centric models of AI ethics to improve public perceptions of AI technologies, how can AI actors respond to the dual forces of human affectivity and rationality in their decision-making processes?

Earlier analyses have pointed to the crucial distinction between popular *narratives* of threats and *actual* risks determined with scientific evidence. While current efforts have tried to achieve AI safety assurances with standards and certifications,[103] there is still ample room for participatory regulatory approaches to transform common misconceptions into more accurate public understanding

---

[100] Aihwa Ong and others, 'Cultural Citizenship as Subject-Making: Immigrants Negotiate Racial and Cultural Boundaries in the United States [and Comments and Reply]' (1996) 37 *Current Anthropology* 737.

[101] Knowles and Richards, (n 86).

[102] Gerdes, (n 64); Berberich, (n 60).

[103] Kurohi, (n 79).

of existing AI capabilities.[104] Employing different communication styles to address human mistrust towards AI depends on a common language accessible to the public.[105] In addition to disseminating facts, key decision parties have to work on countering the mainstream narratives represented in popular media that show AI technologies as leading toward a dystopian future.[106] Against this backdrop there have been policy narratives of valuing neighbourhood histories during a period of radical technological change.[107] In this picture, AI actors have to build and upkeep relationships of trust with community members to lay down the necessary foundation that promotes broader public confidence towards the institutions responsible for regulating AI – without which community acceptance of AI technologies becomes significantly challenged. In this way, community-centric regulatory approaches also address the potential of trust erosion due to blind trust by aiming to reconfigure public trust to a more accurate and proportional level.[108]

In practical terms, this means AI decision-makers must demonstrate a good understanding of human behaviours and the basic conditions in society (or workplaces, family life, and social spheres) trigger trust erosion to the detriment of social cohesion.[109] The starting point of this regulatory approach leans away from seeing human emotions as vague, inexplicable, or subjective and, therefore, better off excluded from models of decision-making processes.[110] Human emotions are embedded into the psychology of trust and distrust.[111] Affective-driven human expressions are crucial signals of how safe or threatened community members feel in their current living conditions.[112] Where the

---

[104] Copeland and de Moor, (n 36); Macnaghten, (n 36); P Lehoux, F A Miller and B Williams-Jones, 'Anticipatory Governance and Moral Imagination: Methodological Insights from a Scenario-Based Public Deliberation Study' (2020) 151 *Technological Forecasting and Social Change* 119800.

[105] Kasirzadeh, (n 65).

[106] Stephen Cave and others, 'Portrayals and Perceptions of AI and Why They Matter' (The Royal Society 2018) Report https://www.repository.cam.ac.uk/handle/1810/287193 accessed 23 February 2022.

[107] Mark Findlay and Li Min Ong, 'Reflection on Wise Cities and AI in Community: Sustainable Life Spaces and Kampung Storytelling' (2022) 1 *SMU ASEAN Perspectives* 1.

[108] Veronica Neri, 'Community and Trust in the Network Society. The Case of Virtual Communities' in Adriano Fabris (ed), *Trust* (Springer International Publishing 2020).

[109] Sairam, Heddesheimer and Bryson,(n 93).

[110] Kathryn Abrams and Hila Keren, 'Who's Afraid of Law and the Emotions' (2010) 94 *Minnesota Law Review* 1997.

[111] Belli and Broncano, (n 76).

[112] David Chan, 'The Psychology of Trust Amid Covid-19 Challenges' (2021])*SID Director's Bulletin* 6.

presence *or* absence of trust is detected in community spaces, this serves as a litmus test that sheds light on certain 'problem areas' or 'thriving areas' in AI roll-out that require regulatory attention. Shared trust may then act as an *emergent quality* of healthy and engaged social bonding; by contrast, social distrust points to fractured community contexts that often complicate the overall success of AI roll-out.

To further clarify and qualify the motivations for tracking public sentiments towards AI technologies, it is essential to recognize that regulatory action should not treat the emotions underpinning trust or distrust as inherently *truth-yielding*.[113] False perceptions can sway trust judgements as much as authentic and value-laden human experiences confirmed by empirical evidence. As such, there exists an imperative to improve the overall accuracy in individual and collective determinations of what is 'good/bad' or 'trustworthy/threatening' – the onus of which falls on regulators and public entities to cultivate techno-moral wisdom in formulating the AI governance and regulatory agenda with community well-being in mind.[114]

Another assumption that deserves further scrutiny is using affective computing techniques or anthropomorphic mimicry to *engineer* public trust.[115] With robotic hardware and AI software designed with innocent smiley faces,[116] the deliberate portrayal of a 'friendly' agential presence is promoted as a convenient way out of a more comprehensive series of community-centric reforms needed to build public trust in the AI ecosystem.[117] Indeed, the subliminal techniques of humanizing AI to garner user trust edges on manipulation; this move assumes passivity in members of the public, removing the room to apply individual *choice* and collective *voice* to influence the trajectory of AI roll-out. Even if the AI-powered personal assistant is built with remarkable 'humour' and 'personality', the individual user still has no recourse to raise their concerns about their personal data.[118] Without appropriate mechanisms for community members to express their stance towards AI technologies, AI

---

[113] de Sousa (n 96).

[114] Gerdes, (n 64); Vallor, (n 67); Renata Grossi, 'Understanding Law and Emotion' (2015) 7 *Emotion Review* 55.

[115] Jakub Złotowski and others, 'Anthropomorphism: Opportunities and Challenges in Human–Robot Interaction' (2015) 7 *International Journal of Social Robotics* 347.

[116] Mark Findlay, 'Why Do Robots Have Smiley Faces?' *The Straits Times* (29 June 2021) https://www.straitstimes.com/opinion/why-do-robots-have-smiley-faces accessed 15 July 2021.

[117] Zhang, Wong and Findlay, (n 77).

[118] Choo and Findlay, (n 9); Mark Findlay and Josephine Seah, 'Data Imperialism: Disrupting Secondary Data in Platform Economies Through Participatory Regulation' (Social Science Research Network 2020) SSRN Scholarly Paper ID 3613562 https://papers.ssrn.com/abstract=3613562 accessed 2 December 2020.

decision parties will miss out on a valuable source of regulatory insight regarding the conditions under which public trust or acceptance of AI technologies can be extended. Acknowledging the causal influence of emotions in human decision-making would also shed light on public indifference as a sign of disempowerment; as the popular slogan of 'AI for social good' is repeated without the genuine pursuit of community voices, the push for widespread AI-roll out reveal the hidden agendas of private-and-public entities to use AI technologies as an instrumental tool to prolong entrenched power asymmetries in society.[119] For this reason, the presence of participation opportunities alone does not guarantee active or meaningful community engagement. Against public apathy and indifference, AI actors should adopt a more targeted approach to identify appropriate entry points and motivate community participation to counter a chronic sense of disempowerment.

2.4   Summary

This section outlines human emotions as a source of causal influence that shapes individual perceptions and collective judgements on the 'trustworthiness' of AI technologies. The double-edged nature of affectivity is revealed as emotions can activate shared trust by strengthening *self-and-community* identities; however, excessive fear or hatred can also erode the social bonds of trust foundational to healthy communities. The myriad of affective manifestations, including trust and distrust, serve as community-centric signals of 'threat/safety' and 'good/bad', which benefit closer inspection by AI actors to achieve more positive trust outcomes in AI roll-out. The temptation in AI governance and regulatory spheres to invalidate the importance of human emotions – deemed irrational and disruptive – is also scrutinized in this analysis. A challenging task for AI actors is cultivating sufficient levels of emotional and cultural intelligence to supplement dominant modes of rational, scientific, and technical knowledge driving decision-making processes. Whether this means addressing the concerns of civil society with empathy or navigating the role of AI ethics in challenging power asymmetries, the onus falls on AI decision-makers to take on the responsibility to build and repair trust relations

---

[119] One concern regarding the operation of trust is whether it is reasonable to expect community trust towards AI technologies to hold traction over a long stretch of time, since AI tools tend to result from rapid development with relatively short lifespans. Is the 'trust and forget' attitude simply inevitable, as people's attitudes towards AI will invariably be transferred to big companies with familiar brands? See critical analysis on this theme by Bodó and Janssen, (n 7); Balázs Bodó, 'The Commodification of Trust' (Social Science Research Network 2021) SSRN Scholarly Paper ID 3843707 https://papers.ssrn.com/abstract=3843707 accessed 5 July 2021.

in affected communities without expectations that AI-human trust is readily attainable through 'trustworthy' AI engineering.

3.   TRUST AS REGULATION

So far, this chapter has argued for shifting AI ethics, as a regulatory instrument that guides decision-making, towards a community-centric model that pays attention to public sentiments about AI technologies (section 1). Additionally, the double-edged nature of human emotions has been outlined to reveal the causal influences of community identities, public perceptions, and trust judgements (section 2). Despite frequent references to calibrating human trust in community contexts to facilitate ethical decision-making, some key questions remain: should humans trust AI?[120] To what extent can appropriate levels of human-to-AI trust even be maintained?[121] In this final section of the chapter, the conceptual notions of trust will be explored in tandem with the proposed regulatory function of trust in activating participatory technological development processes. A simple visual representation is also presented to depict the complex interplay between healthy/unhealthy social bonding, community, emotions, trust, and ethics, which are key components of the AI governance sphere.

3.1   Why We Trust – Definitions and Contestations

Although widely referenced in regulatory discourse,[122] trust is a multi-faceted concept that is highly challenging to define. Many empirical studies and theoretical works have described trust as a psychological phenomenon.[123] Existing academic literature has engaged with this topic in the disciplines of computer

---

[120]   Adriano Fabris, 'Can We Trust Machines? The Role of Trust in Technological Environments' in Adriano Fabris (ed), *Trust* (Springer International Publishing 2020).

[121]   Veronica Neri, 'Community and Trust in the Network Society. The Case of Virtual Communities' in Fabris, ibid.

[122]   James Butcher and Irakli Beridze, 'What Is the State of Artificial Intelligence Governance Globally?' (2019) 164 *The RUSI Journal* 88. See also 'Ethics Guidelines for Trustworthy AI | Shaping Europe's Digital Future' https://digital-strategy.ec.europa .eu/en/library/ethics-guidelines-trustworthy-ai accessed 25 May 2022; 'Beijing's Approach to Trustworthy AI Isn't So Dissimilar from the World's' (*MacroPolo*, 18 August 2021) https://macropolo.org/beijing-approach-trustworthy-ai/ accessed 25 May 2022.

[123]   Gernot Rieder, Judith Simon and Pak-Hang Wong, 'Mapping the Stony Road toward Trustworthy AI: Expectations, Problems, Conundrums' (Social Science Research Network 2020) SSRN Scholarly Paper 3717451 https://papers.ssrn.com/ abstract=3717451 accessed 25 May 2022.

science, robotics, psychology, philosophy, and legal theory. Using the categories of trust assurances proposed by Israelsen and Ahmed (2019), current regulatory efforts have sought to build trust from key stakeholders in the AI ecosystem in two main modes:

1. Trust as a default outcome of AI's *technical competence* and *predictability*. By ensuring the AI system can do what is needed *and* in a consistent way that the user can forecast, its reliability and functionality make the AI system 'trustworthy' to its users.
2. Trust as a direct reflection of healthy and functioning social/commercial institutions. By implementing regulations conducive to situational success, human recipients are convinced they have entrusted the correct decision parties with the knowledge, power, and legitimacy to make good decisions on behalf of average citizens.

It can also be argued that AI practitioners have started to engage with the element of 'dispositional trust' in their design approach.[124] User belief that AI systems will *generally* act in their interest without deception, coupled with their individual willingness to depend on the AI's functionality across a broad spectrum of situations, are favourable conditions signalling community readiness. However, when system malfunctions or 'misbehaviours' contradict user expectations, this can contribute to negative perceptions that AI tools are manipulative or untrustworthy; the viability of AI technologies operating in harmony with human users becomes compromised.[125]

An accurate grasp of human trust dispositions brings the ethical design of AI technologies out of laboratory settings. AI creators' intentional design of AI tools should also link into the wider contexts of how community members envision using such technologies to solve problems in their everyday lives. Israelsen and Ahmed's proposal of distinct trust assurance categories points to the need for a more holistic consideration of what it takes to build trust. To understand *why* and *how* people choose to trust, it is crucial to adopt a *non-reductionist* approach to bridge potential trust gaps between community members and key decision parties in the AI ecosystem. If there exists more

---

[124] Israelsen and Ahmed (2019) consider this category as dealing with 'long-term psychological traits that develop in a person from childhood' that would inform someone's tendency or predisposition to trust technology (p.5). Applied to this analysis, the direct reference to social conditioning as playing a role (even in the background) in influencing trust outcomes is a further incentive for regulators to focus on external conditions conducive to trust in the community.

[125] Julika Welge and Marc Hassenzahl, 'Better Than Human: About the Psychological Superpowers of Robots' in Arvin Agah and others (eds), *Social Robotics* (Springer International Publishing 2016).

than one pathway to build and repair public trust, the methods of trust production can be used to complement each other (without asserting one as more valid than another). While technical assurances seek to improve robustness, safety or transparency within the AI system, another form of trust assurance is achieved by working in tandem with the targeted users to identify whether AI-based solutions have a suitable location in the host community and what these applications may look like.

With each category of trust assurance being interlinked with another, there is a need to clarify, first and foremost, the basics of *why* and *how* trust judgements can alter or regulate human behaviours.[126] From an evolutionary standpoint, a person's decision to trust another entity outside of themselves is derived from the inherent limits in one's knowledge, skillsets, and power of influence; the gesture of turning to others for assistance recognizes that, without external support, the individual cannot achieve their goals and fulfil their desires.[127] At the same time, however, the reality of human finitude – that we all have limits as individuals and cannot know or control everything – invites a degree of vulnerability in the act of trusting: when person A trusts person B, the former is counting on the latter to act in favour of their interest even without a concrete guarantee of success (given the risk of betrayal as what sets apart 'trust' from mere reliance upon an object or subject).[128] Although this vulnerability embedded into human decisions of trust is near impossible to eliminate, as Adriano Fabris (2020) argues, this risk factor is constrained by seeing *how* (not just *why*) a person comes to believe in their judgement that a subject or object is dependable – even when lacking absolute epistemic guarantee that the desired actions or outcomes will occur without incurring negative consequences:

> [I]t is not so much our need to open up to others, to rely on what does not depend on us because of our limitations, but it is the *reason* for, the *cause* of our reliance that is highlighted here. [...] We trust someone or something that provides a firm point of reference: a point of reference that *we* acknowledge. In this case, we do not have to sacrifice anything. Quite the opposite, what we find here is the benefit— benefiting from a firm point of reference—that we get by confiding in something else and that this *confidence* inspires.[129]

Even if human beings cannot escape the necessity of making decisions of trust and distrust in situations of everyday life, the individual still holds agency

---

[126] This analysis restricts discussions of trust to the scope of using ethical decision-making to build community trust towards AI technologies.

[127] Fabris, (n 83), p.124.

[128] Shane Ryan, 'Trust: A Recipe' (2018) 17 *Think* 113.

[129] Fabris (n 83), p. 124. Emphasis mine.

in deciding *how* they determine whether someone or something is worthy of trust (and the reasons why). If a person makes the wrong judgement, their personal experiences of negative repercussions can feed into improving their subsequent judgements on why, how, and where they ought to place their trust in the future (see more on trust as a communal-based practice in section 3.3). In this process, one can learn to manage their willingness to trust – as formed by habits and past experiences – to minimize unwarranted risks.

The analysis has assumed individual-based frames of decisions to trust or distrust. Yet, it is undeniable that public perceptions and trust judgements are only relevant to AI regulation because these factors hold sway or have power over community acceptance towards AI technologies. In a contrary scenario, matters of trust or distrust weigh less in a community where displays of public dissent are largely inhibited or outlawed. The collective dimension that underpins individual trust judgements has to deal with the power dynamics in operation that informs AI roll-out.[130] If trust indicates group compliance and obedience to the authority in control, such power hierarchies would position voices of dissent as unwelcomed social resistance threatening the status quo or systems of dogma. In this picture, the possibility of trust flowing from community members to the decision-makers in power becomes obstructed. AI technologies deployed into community spaces may become a trigger of distrust rather than the legitimate product of community acceptance and co-creation. In proposing an alternative framework to guide ethical decision-making, the regulatory force of trust is employed to disrupt the agenda of AI governance and bring AI ethics into a stronger community-centric focus. The power dynamics underpinning trust are revealed to inspire key decision parties to strive towards building mutualized and reciprocal relationships of trust across the AI ecosystem (as opposed to coercing entrenched power hierarchies).[131]

The emphasis on ensuring key decision parties, including data-subjects, are connected via relationships of trust bears upon the question of whether humans can have such engagements with artificial agents in the first instance.[132] To echo earlier points, mere reliance on someone or something without the risk of betrayal does *not* constitute trust. For example, the affective component of *trust-turned-betrayal* does not apply when the toaster stops working on one fine morning or when the mobile phone does not connect to the Bluetooth speaker.[133] The failure of these electronic tools to serve their intended utility may cause inconveniences. Still, one is unlikely to conclude that they have

---

[130] Pratyusha Kalluri, 'Don't Ask If Artificial Intelligence Is Good or Fair, Ask How It Shifts Power' (2020) 583 *Nature* 169.

[131] Ibid.

[132] Fabris, (n 83).

[133] Ryan, (n 128).

been 'betrayed' by their once-trusted machines in these situations. Even for some algorithms, such as content recommendation or auto-completing business email communications, it is difficult to imagine a scenario of 'betrayal' due to the narrow scope of the AI's functionality. The AI system is either successful or unsuccessful at delivering the intended outcome, which renders its performance mostly predictable by the human user. However, in cases where AI systems are claimed to have a friendly personality to better cater to their users' specific needs, the risks of unpredictable, inappropriate, or erroneous behaviour contributing to user sentiments of betrayal and distrust seem more significant. For example, the digital personal assistant could cause unintentional offence with a rude remark or misinterpret a given instruction that embarrasses the user.[134]

Although research studies have focused on similar empirical-based scenarios and modelling of how human trust towards artificial agents (such as social robots) come to be strengthened or eroded,[135] it is crucial to avoid the misconception that human dispositions to form trust perceptions and judgements of AI equate to the possibility of AI *participating* in relationships of trust with humans. As Ryan argues, trust is a psychological phenomenon that occurs when a person judges 'the will of the trustee to perform that action, where that action is something about which the trustor cares'.[136] In this case, having a 'will' also refers to situations where the human actor judges the trusted entity (such as AI) as having a will even if they do not. Insofar as the AI system has a *felt* presence – whether embodied or disembodied – detectable by their human users, people may form trust perceptions and judgements using their visual, auditory, or other sensory-based inputs afforded through their bodily encounter with AI presence. This is distinct from claiming that AI systems can exercise their 'will' to extend trust towards the human user or form an ongoing relationship of AI-human trust.[137]

---

[134] James Wright, 'Suspect AI: Vibraimage, Emotion Recognition Technology and Algorithmic Opacity' (2021) *Science, Technology and Society* 1.

[135] Israelsen and Ahmed, (n 84), p.5. See also Hannah Lim Jing Ting and others, 'On the Trust and Trust Modelling for the Future Fully-Connected Digital World: A Comprehensive Study' (arXiv, 14 June 2021) http://arxiv.org/abs/2106.07528 accessed 25 May 2022; Paul A Wilson and Barbara Lewandowska-Tomaszczyk, 'Affective Robotics: Modelling and Testing Cultural Prototypes' (2014) 6 *Cognitive Computation* 814.

[136] Ryan, (n 128).

[137] Pepijn Al, '(E)-Trust and Its Function: Why We Shouldn't Apply Trust and Trustworthiness to Human–AI Relations' *Journal of Applied Philosophy* https://onlinelibrary.wiley.com/doi/abs/10.1111/japp.12613 accessed 25 October 2022.

If the regulatory force of trust is located in its function as the social glue that binds people together despite value differences,[138] another question that follows is whether there is a difference between *trust relations* and *social bonds*. To borrow from Fabris, 'trust is born — as a human attitude towards someone or something that feels reliable — *only within a relationship*. Trust is a *specific quality* of such relationship. It is the way such relationship materialises'.[139] Human users sometimes develop affinities or aversions towards AI technologies, in addition to the social bonding processes that already occur among people. However, the same does not apply to the opposite side of the coin. AI systems cannot initiate social bonding nor extend their trust towards other trustees because they do not have 'awareness' from which a subjective sense of vulnerability is developed in the first instance. Indeed, many have argued that it is neither *possible* nor *desirable* for advanced versions of machine intelligence to develop these psychological characteristics.[140] Given AI's capacity to not only *initiate* but also *sustain* existing social bonds among people, however, it can be argued that AI systems – in demonstrating internal qualities that afford a sense of safety, reliability, and functionality – 'act' in a passive sense for people to extend trust, not vice versa. Without the actions of human actors, AI systems cannot actively sustain social bonds or mutual trust. Yet, it may be too early to conclude that AI's presence in the community does not have a material impact on the conditions of trust and social bondedness among people. Earlier analysis in section 2.2 covered that community trust in offline spaces can erode due to activities in virtual environments highly mediated by AI technologies. As such, AI technologies need not be capable of initiating any meaningful social bond to deserve close regulatory attention.

In proposing a community-centric approach towards trust building, this analysis returns to the nature of community acceptance towards AI technologies as built upon the existing conditions of *interpersonal* trust in the wider AI ecosystem. As Fabris recalls:

> [I]t's clear that an ethical judgement of the machine cannot be limited to the machine as such but should concern all the relations that make it what it is — those

---

[138] Cotterrell, (n 44).

[139] Fabris, (n 83), p.134. Emphasis as original.

[140] The topic of Artificial General Intelligence (AGI) developing a personality or consciousness is beyond the scope of this analysis, but it is worth acknowledging that most AI products currently available on the market have not reached this level. With the speculations on AGI being on the horizon, readers interested in the arguments against the suffering of disembodied minds can see Magnus Vinding, *Suffering-Focused Ethics: Defense and Implications* (Ratio Ethica 2020) https://magnusvinding.files .wordpress.com/2020/05/suffering-focused-ethics.pdf accessed 11 February 2022. Section 11.4 Expanding Moral Consideration Beyond (Live) Animals, pp.221–222.

made by humans, about its design, its build, its programme, its maintenance — as well as all the consequences that such actions, also made by humans, have on the more or less autonomous activity of the machine. In a nutshell, machine ethics can only be conceived in relational terms: that is, considering the relationships, mainly with humans, which they are part of.[141]

Any serious pursuit in building human trust towards AI has to move beyond solely verifying the procedural goodness of technical systems.[142] Even when AI systems have strong performance and can be used to guide human actions and decisions, emphasis should still be placed on the 'human in the loop'.[143] The basic starting point is that key decision parties have distinct responsibilities to ensure the appropriate and safe use of AI technologies.[144] While the AI system follows the criteria and principles according to which it has been built, it has limited capabilities to make the necessary adjustments to its operations to respond to novel scenarios. Since AI cannot choose or alter its design principles, it becomes the human's responsibility to monitor the downstream impacts of such technologies and determine whether minor fixes or a complete overhaul of system design is needed.[145]

Some may criticize this causal relation for over-privileging the role of AI creators in the ultimate public receptivity of such technologies. Assuming technical fixes to the AI system is sufficient to warrant community acceptance risks denying the agency of the human recipients in determining whether such technologies can genuinely align with the goals and priorities of the intended

---

[141] Fabris, (n 83), p.131.

[142] Knowles and Richards, (n 86).

[143] Yuri Nakao and others, 'Towards Involving End-Users in Interactive Human-in-the-Loop AI Fairness' [2022] ACM Transactions on Interactive Intelligent Systems https://doi.org/10.1145/3514258 accessed 25 May 2022; Stuart E Middleton and others, 'Trust, Regulation, and Human-in-the-Loop AI: Within the European Region' (2022) 65 *Communications of the ACM* 64.

[144] Seah and Findlay, (n 75); Mark Findlay and Josephine Seah, 'An Ecosystem Approach to Ethical AI and Data Use: Experimental Reflections' (Social Science Research Network 2020) SSRN Scholarly Paper ID 3597912 https://papers.ssrn.com/abstract=3597912 accessed 9 April 2021.

[145] Fabris,(n 83), p.131, writes:
It is humans, who have to do with machines in many different ways, who are responsible for them ... humans are also responsible for the ways they connect an artificial agent with its environment and with the other beings in it, whether artificial or not: each of whom can act differently, according to different criteria and even in unpredictable ways.

host community. As such, enforcing human-centric control procedures to build trust may amplify other significant and hegemonic forces in the AI roll-out.[146]

> One cannot start from the idea that the human being is at the centre of all relationships with the beings that do not depend on him/her or with the systems he/she has built and programmed. Even more so because, I'll say it again, such systems have some degree of autonomy and so they are not always controllable [...] And then, more generally, one should keep in mind that the very idea of the human being as the centre of all his/her relationships had unacceptable, disastrous consequences. Think of the unrestrained exploitation of the whole ecosystem. That's why, rather than re-proposing a regulatory approach [...] one should completely rethink the underlying ethical perspective that should be taken on, in our relationships with artificial agents. That's the only way to justify our trusting them, as well.[147]

Without challenging the entrenched power dynamics characterizing problematic relationships of economic dependencies across North and South worlds, discussions of AI ethics implementation will only remain at surface levels.[148] At the same time, the potential for AI to disrupt the status quo may equip local or regional communities to rework the wider AI ecosystems with the regulatory force of trust to drive positive changes. Using community well-being and social bondedness to counter-balance the dominant wealth creation agenda, the pursuit of *sustainable* AI-human trust relations becomes anchored to the overarching commitment for diverse human communities to co-exist with nature.[149]

3.2   What Does Trust Regulate?

The calibration of trust *in the wild*, so to speak, identifies areas where trust erosion due to misperceptions may lead to adverse outcomes for AI roll-out. Regulatory actions that rectify the absence of trust within key relationships of the AI ecosystem should not be confused with efforts to erase the healthy scepticism foundational to any rational person's interrogation of which entities are worthy of the decision-making powers delegated to them. In the context of AI ethics, as a framework to guide ethical decision-making, the theoretical and empirical mappings of trust across community contexts can help to regulate the following:

- Co-creation processes that improve public trust in AI's functionality and reliability

---

[146] Whittaker, (n 31); Hao, (n 32)
[147] Fabris, (n 83), p.133.
[148] Whittlestone and others, (n 15); See also Ong and Findlay (n 32).
[149] Berberich, Nishida and Suzuki, (n 60).

- Communal deliberation and open dialogue pathways that strengthen public trust in the institutions responsible for the regulation, advocacy, and supervision of AI technologies
- Educational programmes to cultivate evidence-based public understanding of AI capabilities, thereby promoting an accurate grasp of risks/benefits afforded by AI tools

Although individually significant, these stages are mutually interdependent and thus should not be taken in isolation from one another. While shaped by the regulatory force of trust, however, the above steps of trust-building in community spaces also depend on these assumptions:

- Trust as a critical determinant of AI's public receptivity within its host community
- Trust as arising from the negotiation between affective and rational modes of reasoning that stimulate individual/collective sentiments towards AI technologies
- Trust as a measure of community members' active engagements with participatory pathways to co-design and determine AI's functionalities in community spaces
- Trust as an essential social bonding ingredient across offline and virtual communities, which require non-standardized approaches to mitigate AI technologies' impacts on trust erosion

These underpinning beliefs, as outlined above, play a crucial role in informing the ethical approach AI actors adopt to ensure such technologies are fit-for-purpose and aligned with the host community's goals and priorities. By applying the disruptive force of trust as regulation, the points of intersection between community benefit and AI innovation can manifest through localized variations of AI governance across the globe.

3.2.1 A visual schema/causal frame of trust as regulation

The risks of oversimplification are ever-present in proposing a regulatory model that represents highly contextual and complex dynamics. Nevertheless, this analysis will provide a visual representation to render accessible the extensive theorizing efforts detailed in previous sections. To recap, the central claim of this analysis is the role of trust in regulating ethical decision-making to improve public receptivity of AI technologies in community spaces.

In Figure 2.1 below, the central position of the 'community' is an umbrella term for various communal arrangements. Dashed lines are used to indicate the porous dimensions of communities, where the 'virtual' environment bleeds into 'offline' settings and the 'local' meet the 'regional' and 'global' networks. Emerging from the side of the community is the set of communally-salient values, meanings, and beliefs reflected in community-centric AI ethics formulations. Human emotions are depicted to sit between the two elements to shape communally-salient values, meanings, and beliefs while posing a challenge to the effectiveness of existing AI ethical principles. A dashed line is used to demonstrate the interlinked nature of values, emotions and ethics. Sitting below the full spectrum of human emotions are human trust and distrust, which exert mutual influences on healthy/unhealthy social bonding that could weaken or strengthen the community's longevity.

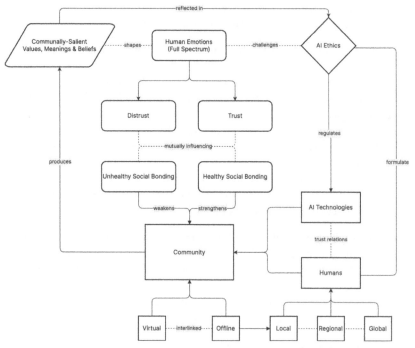

Figure 2.1   A visual representation depicting the complex interplay between healthy/unhealthy social bonding, community, emotions, trust, and ethics, which are key components of the AI governance sphere

Although the causal linkages have been depicted in a simple model, it is worth noting that concrete expressions of emotions, values and beliefs, trust and distrust found in any given community will likely evolve over time. Externalities can drastically alter human behaviours and the activities occurring in the community, as seen through the ongoing effects of the Covid-19 pandemic. As such, when adopting a holistic understanding of how community contexts can be integrated into AI ethics, it is crucial to accept the possibility of community-based changes triggering radical decoupling or stimulating new pairing between emotions, expressions of values and beliefs, and judgements on trust and distrust. The opportunities for community trust to be activated or sustained will also change in response to these externalities. As such, this visual representation should be interpreted as an *indicative* rather than *prescriptive* model of the causal linkages embedded into the construct of the 'community'.

AI ethics sits on the right side of the visual guide as a critical instrument employed by humans to regulate AI technologies. As a decision-making framework, AI ethics receives contributions from local, regional, and global communities; these forms of community constitute the 'human' portion of the trust relation between AI and humans. The visual guide also shows that AI technologies enter virtual and offline community spaces under the direction of AI ethics. The dashed line connecting AI technologies and their users indicates a relationship based on trust and vulnerability from the human side of the equation. Still, whether AI can receive community acceptance based on its functionality remains to be seen.

The answer is simple and complex regarding where trust as a regulatory force sits in this visual representation. To start, the regulatory force of trust connects human actors from the different levels of the community to formulate AI ethics that reflect ethical plurality. The value of trust as a regulatory force is providing a community-centric framework to drive decision-making processes; phrased differently, *trust as regulation* is not one specific prescription but an alternative mode of thinking that disrupts the existing status quo top-down governance approach in favour of ground-up efforts to cultivate healthy social bonding in the community towards AI's social embedding in a sustainable future.

Trust can also be interpreted as flowing through every stage of the causal linkages in the visual representation. As trust starts and ends with the community, effective AI governance strategies may require a more dynamic approach in mapping out wherever there may be regulatory blockages or blind spots that form reservoirs of community distrust that erode social cohesion. Subsequently, trust calibration, repair, and maintenance can ensure the legitimacy of the decision-making processes required to improve public sentiments toward AI technologies.

In short, trust is simultaneously the *context for* and the *goal of* regulation. The presence of public trust serves as the ideal outcome of AI governance while providing additional contexts for AI regulators to monitor the progress of ethical and responsible innovation practices in the AI ecosystem. The regulatory function of trust, then, is located in its influence over human behaviours in situations where trust, or distrust, holds decisive sway over desired outcomes.

As such, trust is not a passive technical quality internally contained within AI technologies – or a certification process undertaken by experts, wherein the role of community voices is devalued almost to the point of irrelevance.

3.3   Trust as a Communal-based Practice on Maintenance, Erosion, and Repair

Incidentally, translating the theory of trust building into practice brings the analysis back to a core theme explored at the start of this chapter: community-centric ethics. Since trust is a relational quality found in social connections across virtual and physical community spaces, AI decision parties face a distinct challenge in addressing the manifestation of distrust. Even if public fear and anxiety towards AI may be inevitable, Neri urges optimism:

> [S]uch uncertainty is not necessarily negative, as it actually keeps us watchful and suggests a few ethical considerations by strongly recalling the concept of joint responsibility in a boundless communication … a sort of communal citizenship that needs active participation to give support but also needs strength and a push to act for itself and for others, as part of a system that acts in real time.[150]

The goal of using trust as a regulatory device is not to completely overpower distrust and the negative connotations associated with its presence (e.g., social division, political instability, fragmented attitudes towards critical institutions of the community). Instead, accepting that human trust towards AI will always be fraught with contestations, the regulatory force of trust positions AI ethics as an instrument that actively engages people – the AI creators, regulators, and civil society – in taking up their joint responsibility to maintain community trust. Sites of resistance and dissent present a further call to action to re-evaluate, repair or reforge social ties that have become strained or neglected over time. As such, trust should be recognized as operating in its *verb* form, that is, as a communal-based practice that regulates and restrains the influence of misperceptions and public fear towards AI technologies.

The ongoing process of fostering community acceptance towards AI based on existing trust levels among the public and key decision-makers is a reminder that AI's meaningful social embedding draws from a sustained and collective effort to negotiate ethical priorities:

> [E]thics, as we have seen, is the way we define our relationships based on criteria and principles that can be shared by all rational beings. Therefore, it is from an ethical perspective that the forms and conditions to give and govern trust can be

---

[150]   Neri, (n 108), p.143.

established [...] The forms and conditions I am speaking of are, then, those that are established by relational ethics: ethics that is focused on the relationship between two or more terms, not just one of them, and that, in the ways such relationship is formed, finds the criteria to guide the actions of human beings and artificial systems alike, and to judge it. Only on this basis can a bond of trust be eventually created, and trust itself can prevail over fear.[151]

Effective maintenance of trust relations requires individual *and* collective practice, without which shared trust can quickly erode and slide into apathy or distrust. Previous research on human-robot interactions indicates that people's decisions to trust tend to develop across different stages, including *learned trust*.[152] Making better trust judgements and articulating conditions of trust, to echo earlier points, depends *initially* on public members having ready access to factual information about AI technologies. A secondary consideration is having communication pathways to capture and document sources of community scrutiny over what, who, and why they *choose* to trust (or distrust) key decision parties in the AI ecosystem to make the right call and steer technological innovation closer toward social good. If AI technologies can facilitate wider community participatory processes, its presence transforms from a regulated object – often labelled as public enemy number one – into something which can achieve public benefit when used appropriately. As a criterion guiding ethical decisions, community-centric forms of AI ethics help to rehabilitate trust relations between AI and humans, among different peoples, and across major AI decision sites.

In this analysis, AI ethics represents a deeper commitment by the individual and the collective to make decisions that build *resilient* and *sustainable* trust relations. Since no person is an island in and of themselves, they have a direct stake in the conditions of trust relations in their communities; therein lies their personal responsibilities to participate in ethical decision-making to safeguard community well-being. To be a person is to assume a place in an existing community of all persons, where the individual emerges from a historical past and evolves towards a future still entangled with the 'associated obligations and claims' of their social community.[153] It is by 'the affirmation of other centres of being, through recognition, justice, and love' that any person's dignity becomes manifest.[154] As such, if social encounters with other persons are fundamentally constitutive of the individual's *self-and-community*

---

[151] Fabris, (n 108), pp.134–135.

[152] Zhang, Wong and Findlay, (n 77).

[153] Walter Schweidler, 'On the Ontological Status of Trust: Robert Spaemann's Philosophy of the Person as a Promise' in Adriano Fabris (ed), *Trust* (Springer International Publishing 2020), p.119.

[154] Ibid.

identity, what is at stake in a person's ability to trust something or someone is their ability to trust in themselves. Located at the core of approaching trust as a communally-based practice is the task of fostering social bondedness – with or without the facilitation of AI technologies – as a collective effort that leads to longevity, prosperity, and continued flourishing of the individual and their wider social communities.[155]

3.4   Summary

The third section of the chapter outlines the value of reviewing *why* and *how* people choose to trust in a holistic way beyond traditional laboratory environments. Rather than formulating a specific recipe to 'manufacture' trust into AI systems, this analysis identifies the critical links between AI ethics and the dynamic operations of trust in community spaces. The incentive to integrate community voices into decision-making pipelines via participatory pathways is also revealed: through participatory design, ethical responsibilities can be cascaded across the AI ecosystem to foster appropriate levels of public trust towards key decision parties.[156] A visual frame of the causal linkages between community, ethics, and emotions is also provided to depict how these components of trust can trigger behavioural change resulting in desired regulatory outcomes. Ultimately, trust is proposed as a communal-based practice that requires public deliberation, accountability, and scrutiny to compel key actors to address distinct categories of trust assurances underpinning community trust. To achieve meaningful social embedding of AI technologies into community spaces, where default interactions between AI and humans are socially *resilient* and *sustainable*, AI actors should consider adopting communally-grounded forms of AI ethics to rebuild trust and mitigate trust erosion – applying the framework of *trust as regulation* is a method of reintroducing a healthy plurality of marginalized community voices into the global discourse around AI governance and undoing the current trend of AI ethics as a predominantly North World project.

CONCLUSION

This chapter has argued that trust serves a regulatory function in determining public response to AI roll-out across community spaces. As trust modulates

---

[155] Ibid.

[156] Findlay and Seah, (n 44); See also Will Orr and Jenny L Davis, 'Attributions of Ethical Responsibility by Artificial Intelligence Practitioners' (2020) 23 *Information, Communication & Society* 719.

individual perceptions and collective judgements, the expressions of communal distrust, in effect, articulate community demands for AI creators, sponsors, and regulators to take appropriate remedial actions. Even when acknowledging trust as a psychological phenomenon, these human behaviours are tied to socio-political and economic-based externalities that deserve closer examination to enable more agile and culturally-reflexive forms of AI regulation. Further empirical investigations are needed to monitor social manifestations of trust across distinct jurisdictions and connect community-centric perspectives with corresponding regulatory environments, to trigger necessary disruptions to the status quo of the AI governance agenda.

It may be true that the ideals of community-centric AI ethics risk placing too much burden on public members to be responsible for the overall trajectory – with all the potential successes and failures – of AI roll-out into community spaces. What if the public is not interested or does not have the luxury of time to participate in board meetings without proper compensation? Does the public even have sufficient knowledge to influence positive changes effectively? It is unlikely that every member of the same community, not least across *different* communities, will be equally motivated to participate. But these reservations do not discount the importance of leveraging participatory governance to create AI's social embeddedness in communities. As the exclusion of community voices could undermine public trust towards key decision parties,[157] any opportunities for data-subjects to articulate their perspectives in the form of open knowledge exchange can defuse anxieties during rapid technological change. Leveraging individual and collective *choice* in co-creation will help to identify the social values and purposes of AI technologies shaping the living conditions of many communities.

As the AI ecosystem overlaps with socially, culturally, and geographically diverse communities, applying trust as a regulatory force to drive community-centric AI ethics will inevitably confront significant challenges. As Roger Cotterrell (2006) explains, stability in regulation requires the fulfilment of two requirements seemingly at odds with each other:

> [L]egal theory (is presented) with a dilemma: how to reconcile in legal thought the demands of the universal and the particular, the global and the local, the consequences of a wide range of both transnational and intranational forces shaping law [...] how to redefine the relationship between the political and moral bases of law's authority in an era when a nation state of individual subjects of a legal sovereign appears less and less the typical, or adequate, locus of the social for law. The most

---

[157] Wee and Findlay, (n 30).

pressing task for cooperation between legal philosophy and legal sociology is to develop theory appropriate to these conditions.[158]

In the context of AI ethics, there is a need to respect every community's autonomy to formulate their regulatory approaches while, at the same time, facilitating a cohesive global picture of AI governance that embodies ethical pluralism and diversity of thought. In this picture, the role of law is to serve as a communal resource to support these communities in expressing their aspirations for where the local and global futures of AI technologies should progress. Active appreciation of diverse communal arrangements where trust manifests, in effect, reframes high-level regulatory considerations into localized forms of ethical decision-making processes: within private corporations' decisions on which start-ups to fund; in classrooms where aspiring engineers learn to build emerging technologies that contribute to social good; in news reporting and online forums where the public engage in debates about what AI should or should not do.

The overarching goal of AI and human communities' symbiotic co-existence clarifies the role of AI ethics: it is a regulatory instrument that negotiates shared trust in the AI ecosystem to connect people with people, communities with communities, and humans with AI. Continual emphasis on the communal nature of these public engagements is deliberate, as the spirit of social togetherness engendering inter-community regulatory action requires a critical distance from the neoliberal rhetoric of self-autonomy and self-interest. By accommodating reasonable pluralism in ethical issues posed by AI,[159] this analysis resists the collapse into moral subjectivism by disallowing individual expressions, whether emotional or rational, to act as the *sole* determination of rightness and wrongness. Instead, one's ethical compass is inherently shaped by their surrounding community contexts – linking to the normative conditions that enable or inhibit the manifestation of mutual trust in social relationships across diverse communities. As such, the role of community remains central to this chapter's proposal of AI ethics as a decision-making framework geared towards building socially sustainable AI-human interactions. When undertaken seriously, the ethical responsibility to steer ethical AI roll-out positions trust as the universal fulcrum upon which scepticism and optimism towards AI-human symbiotic co-existence are carefully balanced.

The conscious loop of trust-building as a communal practice (section 3) back into community-centric ethics (section 1) creates a full circle in the core arguments presented in this chapter. In proposing the requirement for

---

[158]   Cotterrell, (n 43), pp.43–44.
[159]   Audard, (n 95).

AI ethics to reflect the diversity of lived experiences across communities, the onus shifts to the key decision parties to establish appropriate regulatory mechanisms for participatory co-creation in AI development phases. When community members are engaged in public deliberation, their articulations of the pre-conditions to trust create pressure on AI practitioners, regulators and lawmakers to apply AI for social good – not only to strengthen healthy social bonding between people; or rebuild trust among diverse communities; but to create future possibilities for AI-human collaborations to become a disruptive force that challenges existing status quo and other problematic relationships of power or economic dependencies. This chapter has deliberately shifted AI ethics from abstract principles and legal compliance exercises to advocate for maintaining social relationships of mutual trust between people as *necessarily prior* to AI 'trustworthiness'.

The dual mediation of affectivity and rationality underpinning human judgements has also been revealed to be a powerful catalyst driving trust and mistrust outcomes. The visual framework depicting the causal factors that influence community acceptance of AI roll-out has been intentionally broad to invite more specific applications across distinct environments. Because local communities are so diverse, there are bound to be crucial factors impacting ethical decision-making that have yet to be included in the visual framework. Readers, practitioners, and anyone interested are welcome to engage further – theoretically and empirically – with this chapter's proposal of *trust as regulation*, especially with generating refutations or alternative perspectives regarding the undercurrent themes found in this chapter:

• Community, identity, ethical responsibilities
• Public deliberation, moral emotions, rationality and affectivity
• Rhetoric, misinformation, social media, algorithmic fairness
• Trustworthiness, trust, participatory regulation
• Ethics, political and social theory, law and governance

Admittedly, some may find little comfort in the precariousness of trust characterized in this chapter. In an increasingly interconnected world, the widespread sentiments of societal division signal a difficult road ahead for trust-building to be initiated in any meaningful or sustainable way. Yet, if the community spirit of togetherness and solidary can be directed into AI governance initiatives, the presence of AI technologies in community spaces may be altered: instead of an imposing threat, AI innovation can be a vehicle to pursue goals for community benefit. In addition to the commitment to participatory AI governance, the intellectual openness to engage with trust as a communal practice may reveal the possibility for communal dialogue to negotiate AI futures. Once again, this position is distinctly different from asking people to have blind trust in government administrations or technology companies. Just as algorithms have taken public blame for errors,[160] our attention must shift to hold accountable the human actors responsible for using AI to cause damage to individual and communal well-being.[161]

Confronted with the trend of outrage, controversy, and trust erosion in digital spaces,[162] some may wonder if the solution – a way to eliminate the psychological vulnerability of being human – can be found in logic and strict rationality. Nevertheless, there is danger in applying the same rigid rules that constitute the foundation of programmable machines to human decision-making processes. As Fabris warns:

> [I]n technological environments, ethics — that is, the discipline that tries to govern the actions they must perform by interacting with an unpredictable world, based on principles shared by all rational subjects — is increasingly being replaced by a set of criteria that must be followed in a procedural manner. Therefore, codes of rules are replacing moral reflections. Abstract, general rules are mechanically applied to any particular circumstance. In other words: even in terms of actions, it seems that, if you want to act well, you only have to follow the procedure on the right terms.[163]

What is sacrificed here is the full appreciation of *mutability* as a human trait that enables quick responses to ambiguous contexts without pre-determinations, which signifies the full complexity of human intelligence (in the sense of being able to negotiate between strategic, instrumental and emotional aims at once).[164] As such, any general discomfort towards the affective dimension of ethical decision-making should be confronted and resolved. If one accepts the reality that human emotions hold a significant degree of influence over trust perceptions and judgements, even against the persuasion of scientific evidence, this should cultivate a healthy scepticism towards 'the correctness of any particular instance of emotional judgment'.[165] This attitude is quite different from cynicism, as de Sousa clarifies,[166] especially when grounded by the firm commitment to pursue AI for social good. Emotional progress, as contributing towards ethical progress for the individual and collective, provides a cautious optimism that building trust across diverse communities is

---

[160] Sofia Olhede and Patrick J Wolfe, 'Blame the Algorithm?' (2020) 17 *Significance* 12.

[161] Judith Möller and others, 'Do Not Blame It on the Algorithm: An Empirical Assessment of Multiple Recommender Systems and Their Impact on Content Diversity' (2018) 21 *Information, Communication & Society* 959.

[162] Cruickshank, (n 99).

[163] Fabris, (n 83), p.130.

[164] Ibid., p.127.

[165] de Sousa, (n 96), p.124.

[166] Ibid.

a challenging but attainable goal. Against the utopian ideals of a harmonious AI-human coexistence globally, the proposal of *trust as regulation* need not be perfect to be worth consideration.

3. Disrupting data – digital self-determination[1] [2]

OVERVIEW

Data is regularly produced by people. Data can be seen as messages between people and in that sense their transaction forms social bonds in data communities.[3] The phenomenon of social media platforms has created an insatiable desire to share personal information across chat groups and in so doing, due to the terms of membership and use, enabled the platforms to transform and marketize personal data into what they determine as business data.[4] Through this transit, the control of the data-subject over their personal data and its circulation within a designated friendship community is dissipated. The alienation of personal data in such circumstances is much more than a question of privacy. It is a process that fundamentally undermines the ability of data subjects to create and contain their digital personalities, and to ensure that their data messages retain the integrity intended for their original limited communication.[5]

---

[1] The author wants to recognize the detailed and time-consuming work dedicated to the referencing of this chapter by Sharanya Shanmugam and Willow Wong. This research is supported by the National Research Foundation, Singapore under its Emerging Areas Research Projects (EARP) Funding Initiative. Any opinions, findings and conclusions or recommendations expressed in this material are those of the author(s) and do not reflect the views of National Research Foundation, Singapore.

[2] 'International Network on Digital Self-Determination: Concept Note' (2021). Available at: https://idsd.network/ accessed 22 April 2023.

[3] For the purposes of this chapter, and the dynamics of digital self-determination, reference to data does not include digital information either that does not relate to a human data subject or that is not produced by human data-subjects.

[4] Kalev Leetaru, 'What Does It Mean For Social Media Platforms To "Sell" Our Data?' *Forbes* (15 December 2018) https://www.forbes.com/sites/kalevleetaru/2018/12/15/what-does-it-mean-for-social-media-platforms-to-sell-our-data/?sh=4ce0dd942d6c accessed 22 April 2023.

[5] Mark Findlay and Nydia Remolina, 'The Paths to Digital Self-Determination – A Foundational Theoretical Framework' (April 22, 2021) SMU Centre for AI & Data Governance Research Paper No. 03/2021 https://ssrn.com/abstract=3831726> or http://dx.doi.org/10.2139/ssrn.3831726 accessed 22 April 2023.

The revolution that is digital commerce relies on the commodification of data, and personal data is a core in this trade. The proliferation of personal data produced in so many routine and mundane daily social and market relationships, exposes data-subjects to a cascade of data re-use about which they are regularly ignorant and from which they are chronically disengaged.[6] So vast is this personal data trafficking and so complex its webs, that conventional personal data protection paradigms through qualified rights creation are becoming antiquated.[7] If the integrity of personal data is to rest on the active knowledge of the data-subject and some litigated enforcement institutions and processes, then the myriad data transactions which exponentially evolve from the original data source, uncontrolled by and unknown to the data-subject, neuter a legal rights enforcement model minus the essence of an informed and empowered data-subject.[8]

Much of the recent discussion around ensuring responsible data access continues to radiate from state interests.[9] Paternal regulatory modes that talk of data sovereignty embrace the fallacy that data can be contained by state agencies and controlled by constitutional invocations. For instance, the German courts recognize information self-determination as a right, but little energy has been directed to the oceans of data access where data-subjects lack any information to form the foundation of court-endorsed choice.[10]

Similar problems attend consensus models of ethical practice and accountable open usage. Commendable as many of these initiatives may be, they depend on the willingness of powerful stakeholders in the data trade to relinquish control in favour of data subjects. This is hard to achieve beyond limited contexts of self-interest moving to mutual benefit.

And what of those who wish to create and maintain data ownership privileges? Forget the contention that data is not property and that legal endorse-

---

[6]   Mabel Choo Zi Ling and Mark James Findlay, 'Data Reuse and Its Impacts on Digital Labour Platforms' (October 18,2021). SMU Centre for AI & Data Governance Research Paper No. 13/2021 https://ssrn.com/abstract=3957004> or http://dx.doi.org/10.2139/ssrn.3957004 accessed 22 April 2023.

[7]   Findlay and Remolina (n 5), p.21

[8]   Choo and Findlay (n 6).

[9]   'Data Governance: Enhancing Access to and Sharing of Data' *OECD* (10 December 2021) https://www.oecd.org/digital/ieconomy/enhanced-data-access.htm accessed 22 April 2023.

[10]   Antoinette Rouvroy and Yves Poullet, 'The Right to Informational Self-Determination and the Value of Self-Development: Reassessing the Importance of Privacy for Democracy', *Reinventing Data Protection?* (Springer 2009) https://doi.org/10.1007/978-1-4020-9498-9_2 accessed 22 April 2023.

ment of private property rights is fragile where data is concerned.[11] The simple fact is that data, being intangible, ephemeral and nigh-on impossible to alienate, regulatory regimes reliant on data security in any ring-fencing exercise are doomed from relentless market pressures that want data flows to be unbounded.[12]

So how do we commence a practical and achievable regulatory experiment where data can be employed to disrupt the deviant and destructive forces of personal data market exploitation? Any such experiment should start out from empowering the data-subject and this is where digital self-determination (DSD) is both novel and effective. In the section to follow DSD will be described in terms of its constituent elements. With that explained, the chapter will progress to a simple and brief power analysis that disrupts current pathways of data exploitation by dispersing power back to the data-subject and her communities. To achieve this rehabilitated location for data management, it is necessary to build and protect safe (trustworthy) data spaces in which respectful engagements between data access stakeholders can progress.

Specifically, the chapter will explain DSD, pose some questions that might contest its possibility in the mind of the reader, address the importance of safe data spaces and respectful data engagement, look at a formula for enabling DSD, and conclude with a discussion of motivations for stakeholders with different power bases and sometimes conflicting interest. The message of the chapter is that the mutualizing of interests around data access is best achieved through respectful engagement where the data-subject is actively included.

DSD AND DISRUPTION

The disruptive dimension of DSD is through not denying data power asymmetries by creating impotent rights aspirations, or by trying to return data to silos when the concept of data transgression has morphed into mass data sharing,[13] but rather getting back to who creates the data in the first place and who therefore should have first shot at its management. Digital self-determination

---

[11]   Jannice Kall, 'The Materiality of Data as Property', *Harvard International Law Journal Frontiers* 61/2020 https://harvardilj.org/2020/04/the-materiality-of-data-as -property/ accessed 22 April 2023.

[12]   Cason Schmit, Brian N Larson and Hye-Chung Kum, 'Data Privacy Laws in the US Protect Profit but Prevent Sharing Data for Public Good – People Want the Opposite' *The Conversation* (30 August 2021) https://theconversation.com/data -privacy-laws-in-the-us-protect-profit-but-prevent-sharing-data-for-public-good -people-want-the-opposite-166320 accessed 22 April 2023.

[13]   Elia Zureik, Lynda Harling Stalker, Emily Smith, David Lyon & Yolannde Chan (eds.) *Surveillance, Privacy and the Globalisation of Personal Information* McGill-Queens University Press (2010).

is a fundamentally disruptive regulator because the data subject is principally empowered. She does not have to rely on rights, or laws, or best practice to give her a seat at the regulatory table. Instead, because data security protection/ enclosure imperatives are being pressured by market forces for data access and derivative use the regulatory atmosphere is prepared to tolerate and encourage strategies that see:

- power is redirected to the data-subject initially through correcting information deficits
- powerful data holders, users and marketers are willing to concede power in that direction for self-interest such as reputational benefit, data integrity, and trusted data access; and
- the language of data access and trading shifts from concealment and exploitation to respectful and responsible co-creation.

At this point some readers might be circumspect. Perhaps the most significant counter to this disruptive direction proposed is in the nature of data access and transaction in modern social and market settings. If data is always created and sent by one data-subject to another individual or an identified community, and the subsequent data use and re-use is easily identified, and the parties involved cooperate with the DSD frame, then the outcomes in terms of power dispersal would be easy to trace and confirm. But this is not how some data markets evolve and operate. Data use can be layered and multi-dimensional, with transactions shooting off in all directions. A linkage analysis applied to such a complex data tapestry would not be an easy task. This is why the realist advocate of DSD concedes that it should operate in parallel with other data regulatory frames which are designed to deal with data transactions that require staged regulation and could involve significant regulatory opposition from stakeholders.[14]

DSD is therefore constrained by the willingness of stakeholders to participate, and in so doing on the capacity to identify these stakeholders and their data links. Rather than being a major failing in the DSD frame, it is important to recognize the limitations and re-adjustments in information sharing and stake-holder mutualized interests as key contextual variables for the claim about regulatory disruption. While many data webs are complex and may not be well suited to DSD, many are not. Later in the chapter willingness to participate will be elaborated, and a predisposition to information sharing rather than clandestine trading will be offered.

---

[14] These frames could include governed self-regulation and best practice between data-rich organizations and markets, harder command and control legal regulation sponsored by state agencies, rights protection models and civil society intervention.

WHAT IS DIGITAL SELF-DETERMINATION?

Digital Self-determination is a novel concept of constitutional self-regulation[15] that approaches responsible data access *away from rights, sovereignty and ownership*.[16] Instead, it centres on empowering data-subjects in safe (trust-worthy) digital spaces. As the theoretical foundations of DSD begin to find grounding in contextual applications,[17] it is important to clarify the key factors that differentiate DSD from traditional approaches to data access and management.

In seeking to explore a form of regulatory engagement that can facilitate sustainable, and mutually beneficial data access and relationships inside safe digital spaces with a conscious power dispersal towards the data-subject, digital self-determination consists of three constituents:

- *Digital* – the digital world is where this data is largely transacted, even often shifting seamlessly between virtual and actual data spaces. DSD is located in digital spaces and deals with data management across digital arrangements and relationships. It ensures beneficial access relationships around data that are respectful. The creation of SAFE DATA SPACES is necessary for data-subjects to manage and transact their data and that of their communities.
- *Self* – DSD is focused on the data-subject, but it is not limited to an individualist or egoist notion of 'self'. Rather as data is created *between* individuals the data-subject's community has duties and responsibilities to each other. The 'self' centralizes on the idea of empowering the data-subjects in their data communities, to oversee their sense of self in the digital sphere. DSD focuses on more than individualist autonomy – *if data is essentially messages between people, then it will always be relational.*
- *Determination* – Data-subjects are the centre of data management policy and need information about their data to control it. DSD works for the informed transaction and management of data in mutually beneficial arrangements. DSD involves informed choice and being given the opportunity to make actual and genuine data decisions. Data-subjects and their communities become the first line of data access, management and use.

---

[15]   Julia Black 'Constitutional Self-Regulation' (1996) 59(1) *Modern Law Review* 24–55.

[16]   Findlay and Remolina (n 5), p.24

[17]   Nydia Remolina, 'The Role of Financial Regulators in the Governance of Algorithmic Credit Scoring' (March 15, 2022). SMU Centre for AI & Data Governance Research Paper No. 2/2022.

SAFE (TRUSTWORTHY) DIGITAL SPACE

Being certain about the safety of digital spaces enabling data access and control is a matter for data-subjects (and their communities). Safety is trusted as well as experienced[18] and if it is to be a condition of data access for responsible data users, then key stakeholders need to be bonded through trust which is cognitive and conscious, more than a general disengaged attitude of compliance.[19]

In the understanding of DSD, openness is the first requirement for safety to flourish. Next respectful engagement between data communicators is essential. A duty to maintain safety is shared by all who engage data within these spaces. External agencies may have a role in 'policing the boundaries' of safe data spaces and the transit between actual and virtual data flows.[20] However, any such mechanical, non-participatory regulatory technology can do no more than ensure the demarcation of safe spaces in which DSD participants should take command of safety.

Safety (and the trust it engenders) should enable data-subject empowerment, where data-subjects are to be the first line of data decisions, and that they are aware of and at least have a say in how their data is used.[21] As mentioned previously, in a world of clandestine platform data re-use, this indeed is a disruptive pre-condition. To be argued later, initial reasons why data holders might offer information and concede power to data-subjects reveal commercial self-interest progressing on to mutualised data access interests achieved through negotiation and collective bargaining.

As for how to construct and maintain this type of safe digital space, recent empirical knowledge (from the use case referred to below) can be summarized into three 'R's:

(1) *Recognize the costs incurred in managing data safety and responsibility*, and this is including but not limited to human costs. The dissipation of these costs comes through trust and respect around data control enabling more and better quality data access and sharing.

---

[18] IPSOS, 'Trust, Safety and the Digital Economy', (2022) https://www.ipsos .com/sites/default/files/ct/publication/documents/2022-07/trust-safety-and-the-digital -economy-ipsos-july-2022.pdf accessed 22 April 2023.

[19] Christine Vatovec and John Hanley, 'Survey of Awareness, Attitudes and Compliance with COVID -19 Measures among Vermont Residents', *Plos One* (2022) https://doi.org/10.1371/journal.pone.0265014 accessed 22 April 2023.

[20] Microsoft, 'Understanding the Difference between Dataflow Types', https:// learn.microsoft.com/en-us/power-query/dataflows/understanding-differences-between -analytical-standard-dataflows accessed 22 April 2023.

[21] Choo and Findlay (n 6), p.19

(2)   *Regulatory oversight to 'police the boundaries'* of data flow in virtual
      spaces. This is also the area where DSD has tighter engagement
      with hard regulation. An example might be legislation requiring that
      data-subjects are informed about third-party re-use.[22]
(3)   *Respect in data management,* where any conflicts that arise should be
      handled with tolerance, so as to realize the potential of mutual benefit
      and trust. Avoiding languages of rights and law, de-emphasizes a liti-
      gious preference to tackle disputation. In the early stages of any DSD
      engagement, it is likely that there will be difficulties in transiting from
      social and market arrangements for data infected by distrust, to an
      atmosphere of comity. It is expected that this will be achieved through
      socialization where the parties realize the need to shift from shared risk
      to shared fate where data sharing is concerned.[23]

So, who should be in charge of creating the safe digital spaces, or shaping the
trustworthiness in say open finance environments (the subject of the use case
below), if indeed anyone above others? As DSD moves from an exciting possibility to mainstream regulatory policy the nature and attribution/distribution of
responsibility (for trust and safety) and duties (to govern the respectful forms
of engagement) will not necessarily be universal declarations or conditions
of entry. DSD is a self-regulatory model and parties will apply it in particular
contexts with their tailored rules of engagement under a broad umbrella of
agreed terms and outcomes. The role of various stakeholders is still up to the
legitimate expectations of data-subjects and data users to negotiate, but no
doubt cross-border, and public and private sector collaboration are important.
In this vein, maintaining safe digital spaces is not just an over-arching organizational management issue. Safety is also the duty of the entire data ecosystem
to uphold collectively. Ecosystem thinking, based on constructive communication pathways has a strong potential for facilitating other AI regulatory
endeavours such as ethical compliance.[24]

BEYOND SAFE (TRUSTED) DIGITAL SPACES

For the implementation of DSD in open information contexts, there is more
required than having safe digital spaces. For a start, data users need to adopt

---

[22]   Findlay and Remolina (n 5), p.28
[23]   Ibid., p.31
[24]   Mark Findlay and Josephine Seah, 'An Ecosystem Approach to Ethical AI and
Data Use: Experimental Reflections' (December 27, 2020). IEEE/ ITU International
Conference on Artificial Intelligence for Good http://arxiv.org/abs/2101.02008
accessed 22 April 2023.

a preference for transparent decision-making. It might have been thought that powerful data operations would resist transparent accountability to data-subjects. However, to varying degrees the open finance use case reveals that even where tradition has contained customer data behind shields of secrecy, the reputational value of openness, has shifted the mind-set in favour of a more informed data-subject. [25]

Re-iterating, as a bottom-up process of data governance, DSD crucially involves the dispersal of power and control to data-subjects. If this is to be achieved the mind-sets of powerful stakeholders need to change. But without such a transition in thinking, data-subjects will not trust the engagement over data and that the information it produces is the whole story. The more an atmosphere of openness is achieved, the more trust will be generated, and power will be dispersed as an organic market/social consequence.[26] The pay-off for the powerful stakeholders will be realized in more openness from data-subjects and a greater willingness on their part to share data in return and accept openness as genuine.

As steps along the way to achieving a trusted openness, the importance of interoperability and efficiency will be advanced by data marketers. Counter-balancing pragmatic commercial incentives will be the requirement to only pursue these objectives with intentions that do not run against the interests of the data-subject or their empowerment. DSD is an active give-and-take exercise.

Furthermore, DSD also involves fairness in data access to better quality data, which happens through involving data-subjects in valuation and verification processes. If the personal data process is open to the data-subject concerned then there is no better, or more convenient assurance of authenticity. In the era of big data, data quality cannot be sourced through convenient data production chains. Opening personal data once secretly held will ensure not only the integrity of the data but of the data-subject in instances when previously she was little more than a mute bystander.

Finally, the requirement of mutual responsibility in data exchange applying in all contexts where DSD is employed, recognizes the utility of stakeholder engagement in various data exchanges. When mutual responsibility is respect-

---

[25] Nydia Remolina, 'Open Banking: Regulatory Challenges for a New Form of Financial Intermediation in a Data-Driven World' (October 24, 2019). SMU Centre for AI & Data Governance Research Paper No. 2019/05 https://ssrn.com/abstract=3475019 or http://dx.doi.org/10.2139/ssrn.3475019 accessed 22 April 2023, p.32; Christian Ball, 'Why Data Has Become Banks Most Important Commodity' *Global Banking and Finance Review* https://www.globalbankingandfinance.com/why-data-has-become-banks-most-important-commodity/ accessed 22 April 2023.

[26] Remolina (n 25), p.46

fully discharged rather than obligated, then willingness to share will be a further proof that the digital space is trusted.

Something to see policy makers breathe a collective sigh of relief is the realization that DSD can achieve these aims without the need of fundamental regulatory changes in other regulatory fields. DSD as a flexible, consensual and contributory mode can complement existing regulatory regimes closer to command and control, as a form of constitutional self-regulation, which is an added attraction in a world weary of failed regulatory constriction.

ESSENCE, ATTRACTION, PARTICIPATION, COSTS AND SUSTAINABILITY – SOME BURNING QUESTIONS

In this case for DSD as disruptive regulation it is useful, as with any new regulatory approach, to pre-empt some of the concerns that may be provoked by its reliance on power dispersal. The Q&A to follow is offered with that intention.

How does DSD sit with AI ethics as a consensual governance mode? Data ethics is a principled approach to the application of data in the development of AI. Most ethics guideline frames are created by and directed towards those who employ data for commercial purposes, and the data-subject is a passive recipient of ethical decision-making or otherwise. DSD requires safe data spaces in which respectful relationships can be developed around data-subjects and their communities. Ethical data use, concerned to enhance safety and respect is an important agent in ensuring the pre-conditions for DSD. However, ethical ascription does not necessarily require fundamental power repositioning among stakeholders, as does DSD.

What would encourage stakeholder participation in DSD when previously they have thought in terms of data and legal rights? Very simply, more open access to more data with less contestation over the conditions for such access. Currently struggles over data as property, and data sovereignty do not offer congenial resolutions of mutual interests and benefits in data. As mentioned earlier, with the exponential pressure, social and economic, to share data, many current commercial re-use practices are clandestine and potentially exploitative. Unless more mutual and respectful access pathways such as DSD can be enabled, external regulation over data protection will proliferate and contestation will become the default resolution.

How can DSD operate in a communal relationship of trust/duty/respect? Data is neither entirely personal nor entirely commercial/business. It involves the data-subject, the data she generates and how this data flows and circulates within data communities. When the digital spaces for such circulation are safe, data relationships can develop respectfully. Trust between data-subjects and data recipients will emerge in safe digital spaces, there being a duty on both data-subjects and data users to respect data flows and the legitimate mutual interests of participants in data exchanges.[27]

What issues such as commercial arrangements, information deficits and contested interests make the management of data by the data-subject a complicated matter? The negative consequences for data-subjects in much current data marketizing arise because they are not informed that their data is being used and commodified, and as such have no say in whether and how this should happen. Data-subjects cannot even withhold data if they are unaware of what happens to their messages once they are released. Power imbalances in many data markets leave data-subjects open to exploitation. Many personal data protection regimes require data-subject activation and therefore cannot remedy such situations.[28] Contrarily, DSD recognizes that including data-subjects at the outset will not deny data marketing. Rather, it will create responsible expectations governing market relationships and open up possibilities for greater informed access. If this occurs, then the foundations of data marketizing could remoralize the trade away from secrecy and oppression, toward openness and co-creation.

What is DSD beyond data portability and data access? Data portability empowers the data-subject to have a say or some control in the storage and flow of her data. DSD offers a similar facility that is more interactive between data-subjects and data users. DSD may progress no further than informing data-subjects of their data's whereabouts. However, additionally DSD enables data-subjects to have choices in much more than mobility, including how their data is managed in a variety of safe digital spaces in which it resides.

Where is the place for regulators in the context of DSD and what are some of the current regulatory hurdles that DSD faces, if any? Any regulatory regime that works out of a 'data property/data rights' frame will require modification to be compatible with DSD. DSD can run in parallel with such regulatory regimes, but the potential for 'regulation shopping' will add confusion. Personal data protection regimes can be modified to accommodate DSD but will be required to protect the safety of digital spaces and duties for respectful engagement, rather than restrict access based on claimant rights. DSD is an internal, consensual form of constitutional self-regulation. As such, it is distinct from more command-and-control regulatory approaches.

Is there stakeholder resistance to DSD? How can DSD overcome those challenges? There initially could well be resistance, particularly from stake-

---

[27] Lizzie O'Shea, 'Fanon and (Digital) Self-Determination' *Verso* (9 July 2019) https://www.versobooks.com/blogs/4369-fanon-and-digital-self-determination accessed 22 April 2023.

[28] Choo and Findlay (n 6).

holders who are marketizing data in ways that are not respectful of data-subject interests, or responsible in terms of access fairness. But resistance may be based on an assumed loss of market benefit by more open and inclusive access practices. Instead, DSD offers healthy and sustainable data market conditions, where responsible access means more open, trusted and respectful data pathways which should minimize log-jams and contestation when access is suspected and revealed. DSD, if supported, will offer an alternative regulatory option to external command and control intervention.

How could the costs incurred by ensuring data safety and responsibility in DSD be accounted for? Whatever costs accrue from DSD compliance will be more than outweighed by the freeing up of responsible access. This question is similar to the reservations expressed when compulsory licencing entered the market as a buffer to patent exclusivity. What happened in that case was market invigoration and diversification, which overcame any initial loss of property, royalty or licence rights returns.[29]

How would DSD change the global and local outlooks for data access and usage? Since it does not talk the language of property and sovereignty, DSD should not be spatially or temporally bound. DSD works in safe digital spaces, and these can exist in any virtual or actual environment. As such, law's engagement with DSD is much more likely to be at the level of shared norms and values, rather than delimiting jurisdictionally bound trade routes. With the recognition that data is impossible to secure in spatial and temporal confines, and that open access is more likely to stimulate innovation than rights exclusion, DSD is a contemporary agenda for the globalization of data.

How can DSD emerge against weaponization of data and national data interests? States claim data sovereignty for two primary motivations. The first is national security and aligned with that is economic advantage. It will become more and more apparent that national security and economic advantage are more endangered by irresponsible data access (such as hacking through to unregulated trade) than by opening-up personal data to the understanding and management of data-subjects.[30] Pragmatically, nation states can have little effect over data sovereignty when at the same time they seek the benefit of

---

[29]   Petra Moser and Alessandra Voena, 'Does Compulsory Licensing Hurt Innovation?' [November 2010] *Standord Institute for Economic Policy Research* https://drive.google.com/file/d/1X77KMWRI08_BjbZOfO_OUNHqZGCr64PW/view accessed 22 April 2023.

[30]   Erol Yayboke, Carolina G.Ramos and Lindsey R Sheppard, 'The Real National Security Concerns over Data Localization' (July 23, 2021) *Centre For Strategic & International Studies* https://www.csis.org/analysis/real-national-security-concerns -over-data-localization accessed 22 April 2023.

open access.[31] In addition, one of the greatest guarantees of data integrity and responsible data use is data-subject empowerment.

CHALLENGES IN PRACTICE

Recently, the Centre for AI and Data Governance conducted a use case on locating DSD within open finance as it is presently being explored across the global financial industry.[32] Participants in the workshops identified challenges such as complications posed with the secondary use of data, where third-party providers involved in open finance tend not to be adequately regulated, or sufficiently motivated to relinquish control of data so acquired. Questions relating to under what terms data is acquired and stored, and what happens to this data precede determinations on openness and its extent. Such questions can become more complicated with all the different evolving business models in open finance.

Recognition was accorded to a risk in potential trade-offs between different goals for data access and acquisition. For example, there was a tension noted between privacy concerns, and having more open access in financial services, conventionally required to unlock the value creation potential in data. A more basic strain between individual and collective sentiments behind data interests claimed, and different social and economic imperatives often concealed within the expression of these interests might derail initial efforts at mutuality.

Workshop participants were comfortable understanding DSD as striking a balance between stakeholder interests, rather than requiring data-subject pre-eminence. Even so they conceded the need for some power dispersal better enabling the resolution of conflict over data through direct communication and negotiation pathways which make for trust.

There was general agreement about the difficulty in ensuring informed consent in digital spaces from data-subjects to data users, and as such consent was viewed as not acting in some conventional private law form. For instance, in digital commerce and social media, individual users tend to go over terms and conditions with the click of a button not actually engaging with their details as agreed conditions for action. Therefore, it was deemed important to create other consensual pathways safeguarding the interests of data-subjects against rising 'dark patterns' that might be manipulative over their financial decisions. Was DSD that new form?

---

[31] Ibid.
[32] Wenxi Zhang, 'Executive Summary for Workshop 2 of CAIDG's Studio for Digital Self-Determination (DSD) in Open Finance' (30 May 2022) Centre for AI and Data Governance. https://caidg.smu.edu.sg/sites/caidg.smu.edu.sg/files/CAIDG _Executive%20Summary_DSD%20Workshop2.pdf accessed 22 April 2023.

There was some discussion about whether DSD is to be regulated internally through voluntary relationships, and if so who should have that responsibility? Accepting the stark power imbalances in prevailing data relations, who monitors the best practice of the powerful and the conduct of DSD for public good? These conjectures revealed that even in the hard-bitten realm of international finance there was an appetite to consider repositioning power and better recognizing the data-subject. How far this should go might be a work in progress for specific contextual applications, but participants were willing to advance the discussion. Interestingly there was a candid admission that goodwill from managers may not be enough to ensure buy-in. Since data is diverse it will be essential to get specific operational commitments across the data ecosystem. To better achieve a holism towards DSD inclusion, participants wanted both contextual specificity, and some more universal guidelines when it came to apportioning responsibility and duty for access and sharing.

Resourcing DSD was the elephant in the room. Discussion opened up on the nature and extent of infrastructure required for DSD to complement the exchange of data across standardized financial interfaces. It is just these applied questions that drew the research team to devise a formula for advancing DSD, and determining the drivers behind its uptake. These matters will concern the remainder of this chapter.

FORMULA

The proposed formula addresses four main constituents when introducing DSD to a possible application context and its stakeholders:

* understanding the concept,
* describing the advantages of DSD (in this instance for the context of in Open Finance),
* pathways of implementation, and
* challenges going forward.

This 'formula' is seen as applicable for industry stakeholders, data-subjects and their communities and external regulators. For instance, financial institutions might be interested in shaping trust for the reasons of customer loyalty and experience, while policy makers might be interested in trust as a value for social bonding. Data-subjects, as well will look to trusted data spaces being formed so that they have a genuine experience of inclusion. These motivations

DIGITAL SELF-DETERMINATION (DSD) IN OPEN FINANCE

Concept

- Digital – DSD is located in digital spaces and deals with data management. It ensures beneficial access relationships around data that are respectful
- Self – The 'self' centralises on the idea of empowering the data subjects in their data communities. DSD focuses on more than individualist autonomy – if data is essentially messages between people, then it will always be relational
- Determination – DSD involves informed choice and being given the opportunity to make data decisions. Data subjects and their communities become the first line of data access and management

Advantages

- Versatile, can complement existing regulatory regimes in Open Finance
- More open access to better quality data (through having data subjects involved in valuation and verification), with less litigous conflict over conditions of such access
- Allows individual and communal trust to flourish in safe digital spaces; enhances client loyalty and reputational capital
- Makes for mutually beneficial and respectful data relationships that allow for data subject empowerment in a world where marketizing personal data challenges integrity and dignity
- Promotes inclusivity and build financial resiliency for the underserved

Implementation

- Construction and maintenance of safe digital spaces – engaging regulatory oversight to 'police the boundaries' of data flow
- Openness and transparency in data-driven decision making (extent of disclosure to be negotiated between data user and data subject)
- Interoperability, efficiency and standardisation to facilitate the communication of data exchange
- Cross-border collaboration – coordinating public and private players across ecosystems in the fragmented global data policy landscape
- Recognise the costs incurred in managing data safety and responsibility, including but not limited to human costs
- More measures to ensure informed consent of terms and conditions in digital spaces, safeguarding against 'dark patterns'

Challenges

- Complications with the involvement of secondary use of data; increased complexity with what happens to data amid the greater interplay of technologies, and evolving business models and processes
- Potential conflict between privacy concerns (from increased data exchange) and open access in financial services (which help realise its value creation potential)
- Lack of adequate regulatory standards for third party operators; especially with the rising "dark patterns" in digitalised financial portals
- Data users' fear of loss of control from opening access, and insufficient trust in the opportunities offered by the respectful exchange of data
- Geopolitical tensions and data weaponization
- General lack of awareness of digital self-determination

Figure 3.1   DSD formula for Open Finance

can converge in DSD, as the data ecosystem works towards implementation as a co-creation exercise.[33]

As an example, it is up to the industry players with more power over data to ensure transparency and accountability in decision-making, and for policy regulators to exercise some oversight in maintaining the safe digital spaces to guarantee the interests of vulnerable data-subjects. And within these processes, power and control will essentially be dispersed to the data-subjects for them to take on an empowered place in data relationships.

DRIVING DSD

No matter how convincing the argument to this point is, for validating a new regulatory frame reliant on power dispersal and respectful engagement, it is crucial to consider what motivates stakeholders to take up such an opportunity above any other frame. What follows is intended for those who want to participate in a DSD project and would benefit from more detail on how to move from concept to application.

---

[33] 'Participating data stewardship' *Ada Lovelace Institute* (September 7, 2021) https://www.adalovelaceinstitute.org/report/participatory-data-stewardship/ accessed 22 April 2023.

There is much discussion about how to transit digital self-determination from its conceptual understandings, into action. One important component of the central strategy offered by the Swiss Ministry for Foreign Affairs in its recently published 'Creating Trustworthy Data Spaces based on Digital Self-determination' (the Report)[34] is a voluntary code of conduct to guide the development of trustworthy data spaces.[35] The code of conduct, and the achievement of trustworthy data spaces, the Report asserts, require the following basic principles (transparency, control, fairness, responsibility and efficiency). These principles of digital self-determination will in turn represent a governance frame that relies on high standards of stakeholder trust.[36] Even so, the Report does not discount other regulatory forces that can influence data spaces and stakeholder trust.

The Report proposes individual and collective components of digital self-determination. In the 'individual components', it identifies 'knowledge (understandable, clear and useful), the freedom to make one's own decisions (about their data) and the *ability to take action'*. *Taking action* is seen as including the possibility to implement one's decisions in the digital space. Therefore, with principles agreed, and a code of conduct in place, digital self-determination becomes an action strategy – a process that can ensure better opportunities and practices for data management and access in *real-time contexts.*

In 'Recommendations for Action' the Report, while recognizing that digital self-determination can be implemented in different ways, prefers to identify various responsibilities for establishing trustworthy data spaces. In agreeing DSD cannot progress without or outside safe data spaces, context creation is only the first step in an action plan to see stakeholders motivated and ready to disrupt. Accepting the importance of principles and orderly conduct, and drawing from the experience of the CAIDG DSD use case on open finance, the following are offered as potential 'drivers' behind DSD participation.

---

[34]   'Promotion of trustworthy data spaces and digital self-determination' *The Federal Council* (March 30, 2022). https://www.admin.ch/gov/en/start/documentation/media-releases.msg-id-87780.html accessed 22 April 2023.

[35]   We make the distinction between safe and trustworthy data spaces, preferring the former as a more encompassing notion. Trustworthiness, while integral to the idea of safety is not the exclusive determinant. Safety can depend on risk reduction, but more so on responsible obligations arising from agreed duties and respectful engagement between duty and obligation.

[36]   The report does not detail this cause and effect. The work on trust from CAIDG offers some guidance – see: Mark Findlay and Willow Wong, 'Trust and Regulation: An Analysis of Emotion' (June 1, 2021). SMU Centre for AI & Data Governance Research Paper No. 05/2021 https://papers.ssrn.com/abstract=3857447 or http://dx.doi.org/10.2139/ssrn.385744 accessed 22 April 2023.

The concept of 'drivers' is crafted consciously, drawing on the analogy between this action plan and the fact that all computer hardware requires drivers. For the computer, a driver is a set of files that communicates with a computer's operating system to tell the hardware what to do. Motivational drivers communicate with the dynamics of DSD to instruct organizations and communities on data control and management. These drivers, therefore, are both communication pathways and operational incentives for realizing the benefits of DSD.

In setting out a generalized action plan with replicable drivers it is correspondingly important to note the need to 'tailor-make' action strategies to suit the individual communication frames within different organizations and communities. Further, while external facilitation can assist in promoting motivation, for DSD to be inherently disruptive it needs to work on certain already in place organizational frameworks such as ecosystem communication pathways in network-dependent data usage sectors. Accepting the initial stimulus offered beyond DSD, two external facilitators that seem important in all DSD contextual iterations. These are:

- *Data market transition* – market forces and institutional facilities that are amenable to the premises of DSD and do not frustrate the empowerment of vulnerable data stakeholders through pre-existing power asymmetries. Open finance is a case in point.
- *State oversight* – as with the concept of enforced self-regulation, the state should act both as an intermediary to see that principles are complied with, and best practice confirmed. In addition to a monitoring role, state regulators can, if necessary, step in to shore up safe data spaces if the context requires external bolstering.

Understanding these qualifications and pre-conditions it is possible to move on to the identification of individual *drivers for action*. So that this motivational scheme will easily fit into a variety of safe space settings, and to maximize its uptake, the drivers selected are simple, minimal and dynamic. In settling on essential drivers, it is good to be mindful of the criticisms levelled at many principle-based regulatory approaches – that their language is too abstract, too open to interpretation and does not always speak across the ecosystem. In addition, the drivers will need to be sufficiently inter-operable so that they can complement any underlying principles, and evolving code of conduct. Finally, it is presumptuous to impose drivers on organizations and communities that are yet to (as individual data producers) engage with DSD. Mindful of this pre-condition, the drivers are proposed only as optional motivators designed to kick-start their application through *co-creation implementation exercises* with data stakeholders in different safe data space contexts. Co-creation in this

sense means that in each safe digital space stakeholders will actively participate in the suggested approaches to implementation and tailor these to suit the
nature and development of their DSD relationships.

Working with the assistance of regulatory and governance endeavours
focused on safe (trustworthy) data spaces, these drivers can be classified as
operational conditions (incentives) for digital self-determination, and *communication pathways* that enabling its activation as a vibrant and effective
data access and management regime. Fundamental to how DSD can express
and realize regulatory disruption is the recognition that operational conditions
and communication pathways combine to ensure stakeholder ownership. Each
driver should not be viewed as discrete and progressional, but rather working
as an inter-operative scheme to achieve genuine power dispersal and mutual
benefit.

Operational Conditions

Inclusion:
At the outset it is important to identify the stakeholders who have an interest in
DSD in any particular safe digital space, as well as the nature of the data over
which they may have claims, the relationships between stakeholders and the
duties/responsibilities to each other depending on the power they exert over
data in that space. The identification process can be a communal exercise but is
primarily the responsibility of stakeholders with most power over data in that
space and who wish to use that data for any secondary purpose. Once identified
it is necessary to maintain a register of inclusion to ensure that data-subject
interests are adequately recognized and transposed in the DSD process. The
register again should be maintained collectively and managed by the stakeholders with most power over data in that space.

Education:
Once stakeholders are identified and included, they need to be informed and
educated about their data or data in which they have an interest which is held/
used/intended to be used by other stakeholders in that space. The duty to
inform and educate rests with stakeholders who hold/use/intend to use or reuse
such data. A log should be kept by the stakeholders with this duty on how they
have discharged their duty.

Motivation:
Digital spaces can be safe, inclusive and operate with respectful arrangements,
but this will not guarantee all stakeholder participation. Particularly for vulnerable data-subjects who have up until this point been disempowered, ignored
or largely left without trust in regulatory mechanisms, the motivation for par-

ticipation may be challenging. It is important when parties are considering the benefits of participating in DSD, that potential stakeholders make clear to each other what they can offer, as a consequence of participation. For instance, data storers/ providers can provide at minimum to data-subjects information about the personal data they share and how it has been/will be used. Data-subjects in turn, if they are willing to trust data storers/providers may be willing to authenticate their data and open-up further access to personal data for agreed uses. To determine mutual interests as motivations some participants in DSD contexts may settle some simple agreements between parties regarding duties, obligations and expectations from engagement that will also act to further sustain trusted relationships.

Integrity:

DSD is a process that enables data integrity through the protection of the integrity of individual and collective data, ensuring the control and management of such data back to those who created it and determined its original purposes and audience. This is a fundamental and prevailing pre-condition for DSD. A market consequence of data/data-subject integrity is the potential for subject validation of personal data and thereby an increase in the integrity of data down pathways of access. This consequence of the open storage, provision and use of data not only protects the interests of data-subjects in their data but will improve the efficacy of data as it is then accessed and negotiated in agreed data marketing. In this way data integrity and re-assurance becomes a motivation for participation in DSD.

Communication Pathways

Engagement:

DSD is a self-regulatory strategy that depends on the engagement of stakeholders in open communication and negotiation over data. If the engagement is either not positive or respectful, then the digital space is not safe. Engagement, therefore, is crucial to the achievement of respective data interests through data control and management. With the data subject's interests being paramount in DSD the pathways for engagement need to be open, informed and mindful of prevailing data power asymmetries. To promote positive and respectful engagement, the stakeholder 'community' within any DSD context should agree terms such as the preferred medium for communication, nominated contact persons, turn-around time for replies to correspondence and person-to-person communication.

Accountability:
DSD is a dynamic process of communication and compromise. It will succeed or fail on the establishing and maintenance of trusted relationships about data use. Transparency around the storage, provision and use of data is an important factor in establishing and maintaining trust.[37] However, openness alone will not always ensure trust between stakeholders.[38] In fact, openness about data use may initially damage trust until good data use practices are agreed. DSD is necessary because a lack of openness or problematic data storage, provision and use could endanger the possibility of trust when data is transacted. As has been revealed with social media platforms, (such as Tic Toc, Instagram, Facebook) even conditional consent requirements or privacy protocols will not always bring trust.[39] Sometimes even ethical standards, and product safety/risk minimizing will not guarantee trust.[40] Trust, once established, must be continually nurtured and confirmed. Recognizing this commitment it is essential, accountability mechanisms should be built into safe data spaces so that stakeholders with greatest power over data in particular, can regularly be required to confirm that they are complying with the spirit of DSD in their data management practices. This should be more than a tick-box audit. Depending on the nature, extent and duration of any DSD context, stakeholders can agree to nominate a data steward/custodian who will be responsible to ensure that accountability mechanisms are operational and inclusive, providing satisfaction to all parties.

Sustainment:
DSD should be habitual and not viewed as a process for curing already problematic data control inequalities. However, due to the current novelty of DSD

---

[37]   Mark Findlay and Nydia Remolina, 'Regulating Personal Data Usage in COVID-19 Control Conditions' (May 22, 2020). SMU Centre for AI & Data Governance Research Paper No. 2020/04 https://papers.ssrn.com/sol3/papers.cfm ?abstract_id=3607706 or http://dx.doi.org/10.2139/ssrn.3607706 accessed 22 April 2023.

[38]   'Singapore's Data Debacle Shakes City-State's "Smart" Ambitions' *Financial Times* (23 February 2021) https://www.ft.com/content/1cc807c9-9e2b-4dfd-9c11 -54a990bbd2f0 accessed 22 April 2023.

[39]   Marcus Moretti and Micheal Naughton, 'Why Privacy Policies Are So Inscrutable' *The Atlantic* (5 September 2014) https://www.theatlantic.com/technology/ archive/2014/09/why-privacy-policies-are-so-inscrutable/379615/ accessed 22 April 2023.

[40]   Alicia Wee and Mark James Findlay, 'AI and Data Use: Surveillance Technology and Community Disquiet in the Age of COVID-19' (September 14, 2020). SMU Centre for AI & Data Governance Research Paper No. 2020/10 https://ssrn.com/abstract= 3715993 or http://dx.doi.org/10.2139/ssrn.3715993 accessed 22 April 2023.

and the possible resistance to open data relationships in the minds of some stakeholders, sustainability needs commitment. Communities and markets that practice DSD will develop trusted data relations whether these be commercial or social, that will perpetuate more sustainable market arrangements and social bonds where data is concerned.[41] To convince market players and community stakeholders who may have been at odds with each other over data management prior to DSD, that this new approach offers a genuine alternative to contestation, advocates of DSD will need to engage in community/market awareness programmers and consensus-building exercises, to spread the message of DSD to those who would benefit from its operation.

Conflict resolution:
Implementing and embedding DSD will not be without its challenges. As with any data relationship there may be disagreements about who has what interests and whose interests should prevail in any management or control encounter. Indeed, data interests will evolve as data is used and therefore apportioning such interests and seeing principal stakeholders are empowered to enjoy the benefits of their data may necessitate negotiation.[42] So that conflicts over data interests do not derail the respectful and trusted engagement at the heart of effective DSD, there may be occasions where conflicts require resolution.

In the maintenance of safe data spaces, the contextual identification conditions in that space that may lead to conflict should be constantly considered by stakeholders so that amelioration can be attempted before conflict emerges. Such amelioration requires continual, informed and responsive conversations between stakeholders about their legitimate expectations over the course of DSD.

These conversations need to be informed by earlier conflict occasions and dynamics and their evolution. At this pre-emptive stage potential conflicts can be mediated, and conflict-generating conditions can be moderated, building true trust relationships. Data-subjects need to be provided with the information they believe may ameliorate power dependencies and social exclusion on which conflict feeds. Information sharing at this stage is imperative if fear and perceived risk of data abuse are to be addressed.

Most importantly, the 'learning from experience' dimension of conflict is a tool for social bonding as much as a force for disruption, and thus needs recognition. Once a conflict has been predicted and talked through, or identified

---

[41] Findlay and Remolina (n 4), p.27
[42] ECHA, 'The Dos and Don'ts for Data Sharing Negotiations', https://echa .europa.eu/support/registration/working-together/practical-advice-for-data-sharing -negotiations/dos-and-donts-for-data-sharing-negotiations accessed 22 April 2023.

and resolved via information sharing, interest compromise and mutual respect, the experience of the DSD experience will become more trusting.

CONCLUSION

It would be helpful to read this chapter along with our work on trust.[43] In so doing some of the more theoretical and conceptual underpinnings of the relationships to be positively forged through DSD will lead on to wider enquiry into representative, participant regulation.[44]

If disruption is changing the direction of forces at work in the market, then to propose a data-control approach that is grounded on power dispersal from the data holders to the data generators should qualify. What this chapter intends is to first establish the need for such disruption by revealing the destructive consequences of current data access, use and marketizing practises. These effects are destructive not just of data-subject privacy but by undermining the integrity of the data access and use ecosystem of data market sustainability, reliant as it is on trust.[45] Disruptive regulation repositioning power asymmetries at the heart of economic disruption/data disruption is designed to ensure that order can return to data access beyond the priorities only of discriminatory market benefit.

While digital self-determination can be described simply, the analysis would not be adequate if it did not candidly confront limitations and challenges in the approach. The chapter has employed the experiences in a recent open finance use case to specify these challenges in terms of potential stakeholder opinion and industry practice. A formula for marketing DSD is offered as are some general reflections on tensions between context specific ownership and the robustness of certain universal themes. Returning to disruption, the analysis reveals to critical reflection by indicating the dissonance between an attractive data access facilitation scheme and a genuinely novel form of inclusive regulatory practice.

So that the reader with an interest in disruptive data access options such as DSD can dabble in its applicability, the chapter winds up with a 'map' for the motivation of potential stakeholders and the challenging implementation invocations. The map combines contextual considerations that incubate motivation and communication pathways that operationalize mutual interests.

---

[43]   Findlay and Wong (n 36).

[44]   Hanan Haber and Eva Heims, 'Regulating with the Masses? Mapping the Spread of Participatory Regulation' (November 17, 2020) Journal of European Public Policy 27:17, p.1599–611 https://doi.org/10.1080/13501763.2020.1817128 accessed 22 April 2023.

[45]   Findlay and Remolina (n 5), p.27.

The shift in style and purpose throughout the chapter can be given cohesion around the desire not just to present a disruptive regulatory possibility, but to set out the building blocks to enable its adoption and ownership by parties previously very suspicious of each other's motives and intentions. The chapter adopts a powerful theme in all the contributions – that the devices for economic disruption (AI and big data) and the objects of economic disruption (data access and usage) can be turned into regulatory building blocks if the regulatory strategy confronts power asymmetry and dispersal.

In 'questioning of the normative understandings of selfhood, community, and nation, juxtaposed against the territorial, ownership and propertied notions that pervade privacy discourse'[46] DSD challenges core elements of data protection regimes. Present privacy scholarship conventions assume one 'owns' oneself (which is a profound falsehood) – that communities are bonded through aspirations of wealth creation and not critical cooperation and ultimately DSD denies property in data. This is a radical agenda.

---

[46] Payal Arora (2019) 'De-colonising Privacy Studies', *Television and New Media* 20/4: https://doi-org.libproxy.smu.edu.sg/10.1177/1527476418806092 accessed 22 April 2023.

4. Modern AI ethics is a field in the making[1]

By Josephine Seah

ROLLING WITH ITS OWN MOMENTUM

Technologies of artificial intelligence (AI) and machine learning (ML) are becoming ever more ubiquitous in our lives. From healthcare to financial systems, from transport infrastructures to education, the application of ML systems is rapidly gaining ground, presented as solutions to the challenges facing our societies. While it is difficult to deny its potential, a growing body of research has nonetheless increasingly drawn attention to the ways that these technologies can amplify and exacerbate social inequalities. The modern field of AI ethics has developed both in conjunction with and in response to this body of work. Yet given the disconnect between social expectations, profit motivations, and underdeveloped regulations, it is unsurprising that some have called the existing landscape a 'wild west' of technologies. Indeed, the rapid proliferation of AI technologies for content moderation, surveillance, and predictive profiling resembles a frontier space: 'Frontier men and resources', anthropologist Anna Tsing writes:

> are made of dynamics of intensification and proliferation. Confusions between legal and illegal, public and private, disciplined and wild are productive in sponsoring the emergence of men driven to profit, that is entrepreneurs, as well as the natural objects conjured in their resourceful drives. These men and objects are contagious, recharging the landscape with their wilderness and virility. The frontier then appears to roll with its own momentum.[2]

Tsing's words, made in reference to forestry practices in Indonesia, none-theless ring true in the expansive optimism of what AI/ML technologies are

---

[1] Thilo Hagendorff, 'Blind Spots in AI Ethics' (2021) *AI and Ethics* https://doi .org/10.1007/s43681-021-00122-8 accessed 14 February 2022.
[2] Anna Lowenhaupt Tsing, *Friction: An Ethnography of Global Connection* (Illustrated edition, Princeton University Press 2004).

imagined doing: Mark Zuckerberg's belief that AI can 'fix' misinformation and hate speech on his platform stands as just such a recent example.[3] This often-renegade space of AI/ML – evident not just in pronouncements from tech leaders like Zuckerberg, but also in the channelling of public and private funds and resources into research laboratories and national programs and ongoing efforts of governance and legislation[4] – has been continuously marked by thorny ethical challenges. One needs to look no further than the recent controversy over GPT-4chan, a large language model (LLM) released by an AI researcher and YouTuber. GPT-4chan was fine-tuned on a dataset that contained racist, white supremacist, anti-semantic, anti-Muslim, misogynistic, and anti-LGBT views. Unsurprisingly, the model learned to output these very forms of speech. While the researcher who released the model 'strongly recommended... not [to] deploy this model into a real-world environment unless its behaviour is well-understood and explicit and strict limitations on the scope, impact, and duration of the deployment are enforced',[5] the model was nonetheless downloaded over a thousand times. Its release sparked a huge debate among AI researchers on the ethics of developing such models, the harms that come from such LLMs, the associated problems with releasing them to the public, and the utility of building such models to begin with given the known harms.[6] Conventional arguments about AI regulation often cite the need for *balance* between innovation and regulation, as captured in the Collingridge Dilemma, the argument that:

> [A]ttempting to control a technology is difficult, and not rarely impossible, because during its early stages, when it can be controlled, not enough can be known about its harmful social consequences to warrant controlling its development; but by the time these consequences are apparent, control has become costly and slow.[7]

Yet what this instance revealed was not about the need to strike a balance between openness and responsibility so much as the fact that we are now in

---

[3]   'AI Will Solve Facebook's Most Vexing Problems, Mark Zuckerberg Says. Just Don't Ask When or How.' *Washington Post* https://www.washingtonpost.com/news/the-switch/wp/2018/04/11/ai-will-solve-facebooks-most-vexing-problems-mark-zuckerberg-says-just-dont-ask-when-or-how/ accessed 15 June 2022.

[4]   Aphra Kerr, Marguerite Barry and John D Kelleher, 'Expectations of Artificial Intelligence and the Performativity of Ethics: Implications for Communication Governance' (2020) 7 *Big Data & Society* 2053951720915939.

[5]   Andrey Kurenkov, 'Lessons from the GPT-4Chan Controversy' (*The Gradient*, 12 June 2022) https://thegradient.pub/gpt-4chan-lessons/ accessed 14 June 2022.

[6]   Ibid.

[7]   David Collingridge, *The Social Control of Technology / David Collingridge*. (Pinter 1982) 19.

the latter stage of AI development, where controlling such systems has become the landscape upon which arguments are framed. Indeed, if GPT-4chan is any indication, control is proving to be both costly, slow, and socially harmful. For AI Ethics research the problem of impactful governance that ethicists, policy makers and regulators face need to be understood in terms of timescales and risk minimizing. While regulatory principles and frameworks have been articulated, and interventionist legislation increasingly becoming a reality,[8] our near and mid-term futures of engaging AI – still unfolding with the frontier logic of moving fast and breaking things – may yet be continuously interrupted with these incidences of problematic and ill-conceived 'experiments'.

What is the role of AI Ethics? What lessons can be adapted from ideas of responsible innovation such that AI Ethics can be both disruptive and yet *generative* for more responsible and sustainable AI development? This chapter asks how we might support the continued relevance of AI Ethics in discussions of the social sustainability of AI/ML systems. The chapter has two goals: first, to reframe the challenges of AI Ethics. Efforts to incorporate ethics or ethical decision-making into AI expansion are increasingly falling to the design level; and in turn, to the decisions made by practitioners working on building AI/ML systems. Rather than echo these expectations, this chapter reframes the challenges of AI Ethics as a series of individual, organizational, and institutional problems that need to be addressed for it to achieve its disruptive and generative potentials. This flows into the chapter's second goal: to conceive of AI Ethics as a form of generative friction – an intentional practice set in opposition to the forward momentum of technological progress that occurs at the frontier of development and deployment. The chapter argues that necessary speed bumps are required on the road to AI expansion, forming behavioural, organizational, and institutional points of frictions across the ML production pipeline and stresses the need for more research on cultural contexts and organizational incentive structures that configure the ways in which practitioners, designers, and developers act in responsible and irresponsible ways when advancing AI innovation.

This chapter may be useful for regulators unfamiliar with ongoing arguments, initiatives, and efforts from within the field of computer science to address ethical quandaries in the AI/ML field. I draw on research from domains of human-computer interaction, critical data studies, and key conferences – particularly FAccT and AIES – that contribute to continuing efforts to shape the field of AI Ethics and can aid ongoing regulatory and policy discus-

---

[8]   Jeremy Kahn, 'The Sun Is Setting on A.I.'s Wild West' (*Fortune*, 27 April 2021) https://fortune.com/2021/04/27/the-sun-is-setting-on-a-i-s-wild-west/ accessed 15 June 2022.

sions. In addition to their significance for this discussion about responsible AI practices, the arguments presented in these domains are also prescient given this volume's focus on the incorporation of AI/ML models *into* the regulation of other domains – such as machine learning for technical risk assessment or cybersecurity.[9]

The rest of this chapter proceeds as follows: the second section traces the trajectory of AI ethics over the past handful of years. It sketches out recent developments in the field and focuses on key questions that critical scholars currently confront. The section ends by discussing the prevailing relevance of AI Ethics despite its key problems and challenges, identifying essential changes that might need to be made for ensuring that AI ethics remains material and useful in regulation. The following section then presents an argument for an organizational dimension in AI ethics research and provides a case-study of how a change in perspective, expectation, and analytical focus can offer a more productive research direction, proving fruitful for realising ethical and responsible AI innovation. The final section draws out challenges faced by such a repositioning and concludes in its favour.

THE LANDSCAPE OF AI ETHICS

Research looking into the real-world impacts of AI and their potentials for exacerbating existing social inequalities has made a strong case for the deployment of such models to be balanced by stronger commitments towards the goals of fairness, justice, and equity. Since 2015, this interest has culminated in the publication of documents laying out guidelines or principles meant to guide and structure the development of AI. From private organizations – IBM's Principles of Trust and Transparency, PWC UK's Responsible AI Framework – to national governments – Beijing's AI Principles, Singapore's Model AI Governance Framework – and supranational entities – the OECD's AI Principles;[10] and the UNESCO member states adopting a global agreement on the Ethics of AI.[11] The years from 2016 to 2020 marked a rush towards articulating forms of ethical AI guidance. These documents also hinted at a converging set of interests and priorities that would come to set the boundaries of AI Ethics as a significant and common research field. Substantiating

---

[9]   Jeevith Hegde and Børge Rokseth, 'Applications of Machine Learning Methods for Engineering Risk Assessment – A Review' (2020) 122 *Safety Science* 104492.

[10]   https://oecd.ai/en/ai-principles accessed 22 April 2023.

[11]   https://en.unesco.org/artificial-intelligence/ethics#recommendation accessed 22 April 2023.

this,[12] similarly, scholars at the Berkmen Klein Centre compared 36 documents and noted the seeming convergence of a similar set of principles: privacy, accountability, safety and security, transparency and explainability.[13]

Despite the articulation of a set of seemingly similar ethical principles,[14] the operationalization of principles like accountability, responsibility, and transparency have nonetheless proven to be a highly complex task, culminating in what many have come to call the gap between principles and practice.[15] This section sketches out the challenges that make this gap an intricate one to address. I sketch out a series of problems that can be read on a continuum from individual to structural challenges that need to be articulated, researched, and addressed to reduce the gap between principles and practice. While these challenges mentioned are indicative, they are not exhaustive. Ultimately, the section suggests that a willingness to discuss these challenges will enable a better reconceptualization of what AI ethics can productively accomplish – or, in other words, represent a regulatory mechanism that maintains its 'teeth'.[16]

Grounding Principles into Practice

Interpreting abstractions. As discussed above, moving from nominating key concepts such as fairness, explainability, and justice, on to the articulation of these principles in practice remains a key challenge for governance policy. One reason is that such concepts are contested, open to interpretation, and

---

[12]   Anna Jobin, Marcello Ienca and Effy Vayena, 'The Global Landscape of AI Ethics Guidelines' (2019) 1 *Nature Machine Intelligence* 389.

[13]   Jessica Fjeld and others, 'Principled Artificial Intelligence: Mapping Consensus in Ethical and Rights-Based Approaches to Principles for AI' (Social Science Research Network 2020) SSRN Scholarly Paper ID 3518482 https://papers.ssrn.com/abstract= 3518482 accessed 16 February 2022.

[14]   Jobin, Ienca and Vayena (n 12); Fjeld and others (n 13).

[15]   Jessica Morley and others, 'Operationalising AI Ethics: Barriers, Enablers and next Steps' (2021) *AI & Society* https://doi.org/10.1007/s00146-021-01308-8 accessed 14 February 2022; Jessica Morley and others, 'From What to How: An Initial Review of Publicly Available AI Ethics Tools, Methods and Research to Translate Principles into Practices' (2020) 26 *Science and Engineering Ethics* 2141; Morley and others, 'Operationalising AI Ethics'; Javier Camacho Ibáñez and Mónica Villas Olmeda, 'Operationalising AI Ethics: How Are Companies Bridging the Gap between Practice and Principles? An Exploratory Study' (2021) *AI & Society* https://doi.org/10.1007/ s00146-021-01267-0 accessed 17 February 2022; Conrad Sanderson and others, 'AI Ethics Principles in Practice: Perspectives of Designers and Developers' [2022] arXiv:2112.07467 [cs] http://arxiv.org/abs/2112.07467 accessed 17 February 2022.

[16]   Anaïs Rességuier and Rowena Rodrigues, 'AI Ethics Should Not Remain Toothless! A Call to Bring Back the Teeth of Ethics' (2020) 7 *Big Data & Society* 2053951720942541.

require a high level of technical and contextual understanding to operational-ize. For example, while fairness might be an accepted general aspiration across the ecosystem, in practice it remains an abstract ideal: 'mak[ing] the principles less useful for practical purposes and for creating a common understanding of their meaning'.[17] Jobin et al., for example, have pointed out substantial differences in how these ethical principles have been interpreted, justified, and prioritized by different stakeholders, '[t]hese conceptual and procedural diver-gences reveal uncertainty as to which ethical principles should be prioritized and how conflicts between ethical principles should be resolved'.[18]

Such divergences in interpretations and prioritizations point to the range of different expectations and technical solutions that are available to AI practitioners in complying with ethics codes. Morley and her colleagues, for instance, have found over 400 sources that discuss, either theoretically or practically, how to develop ethical algorithmic systems.[19] Yet the multiplicity of available tools has itself been overwhelming for practitioners: Arvan sums this up in his documentation of an ongoing 'moral-semantic trilemma', where interpretations of ethics in tools meant to aid their operationalization have either been 'too semantically strict, too semantically flexible, or overly unpre-dictable'.[20] Indeed, in Morley et al.'s review of existing tools and methods, they highlighted how many of these tools present a high barrier for use: either offering limited aid for implementing them within existing ML production pipelines, or because they required a sophisticated skill level for use. As such, like Arvan's argument, existing tools either limit the manoeuvrability of prac-titioners when they need it, or conversely provide too much leeway and expect too much tinkering and effort on the part of AI practitioners in approaching compliance. These barriers led to their conclusion that the 'overarching lack of usability of the tools and methods [found]… [means that] they require more work before being "production-ready"'.[21] In a similar vein, Lee and Singh conducted a comparative assessment of six open-source fairness toolkits and highlighted gaps between their capabilities and what practitioners needed for

---

[17] Merve Hickok, 'Lessons Learned from AI Ethics Principles for Future Actions' (2021) 1 *AI and Ethics* 41, 41.

[18] Jobin, Ienca and Vayena (n 12).

[19] Jessica Morley and others, 'From What to How: An Initial Review of Publicly Available AI Ethics Tools, Methods and Research to Translate Principles into Practices' in Luciano Floridi (ed), *Ethics, Governance, and Policies in Artificial Intelligence* (Springer International Publishing 2021) https://doi.org/10.1007/978-3-030-81907-1_10 accessed 17 February 2022.

[20] Marcus Arvan, 'Mental Time-Travel, Semantic Flexibility, and A.I. Ethics' (2018) *AI & Society* https://doi.org/10.1007/s00146-018-0848-2 accessed 14 March 2022.

[21] Morley and others, 'From What to How' (n 19).

them to work in practice. As With Morley et al.'s findings, they found in their assessment of the toolkits that they required a rich familiarity with fairness literature; and had embedded within them assumptions of how much control and knowledge practitioners had about the datasets they were working with.[22]

These observations raise practical implications: research with practitioners has highlighted the latter groups' frustration when trying to use these tools and methods.[23] A recent handful of studies have come to similar telling conclusions: that existing toolkits and methods for operationalizing ethics at the design level continue either be too confusing or unproductive for AI practitioners. Holstein et al., for example, pointed to many real-world challenges that practitioners face in their attempts to develop fairer ML systems such as domain-specific education resources and tools that are needed for making toolkits and their methodologies work in practice.[24] In a recent similar study, Deng et al. concluded that practitioners require more support before they are able to comfortably use fairness toolkits in their work.

Avoiding solutionism. These complexities with interpretations of principle matter at different stages of the ML production pipeline. They come into play at the beginning of a project when a problem is being formulated by practitioners and data scientists, through to a model's implementation and testing. An associated governance challenge is the dominance of existing *technical solutions* when approaching ethics regulatory considerations. Sociotechnical systems (existing fairness toolkits, for example), tend to advance statistical models of calculating fairness.[25] Doing so asks practitioners to understand these modes of calculations – an expertise that not all data and AI practitioners possess. Elsewhere, scholars have also noted an unevenness in the principles that tools and methods were aiming to operationalize explicability, in particular what principles had the greatest number of tools available. They suggested that this skew may have arisen because 'the problem of interpreting

---

[22]   Michelle Seng Ah Lee and Jat Singh, 'The Landscape and Gaps in Open Source Fairness Toolkits', *Proceedings of the 2021 CHI Conference on Human Factors in Computing Systems* (ACM 2021) https://dl.acm.org/doi/10.1145/3411764.3445261 accessed 11 June 2022.

[23]   Dorian Peters, 'Beyond Principles: A Process for Responsible Tech' (*The Ethics of Digital Experience*, 14 May 2019) https://medium.com/ethics-of-digital-experience/beyond-principles-a-process-for-responsible-tech-aefc921f7317 accessed 14 March 2022.

[24]   Kenneth Holstein and others, 'Improving Fairness in Machine Learning Systems: What Do Industry Practitioners Need?', *Proceedings of the 2019 CHI Conference on Human Factors in Computing Systems* (ACM 2019) https://dl.acm.org/doi/10.1145/3290605.3300830 accessed 11 June 2022.

[25]   Ninareh Mehrabi and others, 'A Survey on Bias and Fairness in Machine Learning' (2021) 54 *ACM Computing Surveys* 115:1.

algorithmic decisions seem tractable from a mathematical standpoint' and as such 'the principle of explicability has come to be seen as a most suitable for a technical fix'.[26]

This tendency to favour and highlight technical solutions to complex social issues has resulted in the crafting of approaches to AI that '[strips down] the multidimensionality of very complex social constructs to something that is idealised, measurable, and calculable'.[27] The regulatory challenge that arises here is in avoiding an inclination to approach a social problem as programmable and that in turn warrants a technical intervention.[28] Hagendorff illustrates this point using privacy as an example:

> privacy principles aim at protecting sensitive personal information, be it by manipulating datasets in order to obfuscate them or by protesting against AI-driven interfaces. But neither the dataset nor the interfaces are the problem. The real issue is unfair social discrimination and intolerance that renders some information "sensitive" since its disclosure would initiate oppressive measures.[29]

Widder and his colleagues have made a useful distinction here between implementation harms – harms that arise from 'code, algorithm or data problems that can be fixed without changing the intent, or use, of the software' – and use-based harms – harms that arise from a use of software that is in itself harmful. Practitioners are thus not only interpreting principles that are vague, but they are also often learning this distinction between implementation and use harms as they work on their projects.

The Diffusion of Responsibility

While practitioners struggle with interpreting and grounding ethical principles, they are often situated within incentive structures that limit their scope of normative and ethical decision-making. In other words, responsible AI development is plagued by the 'many hands problem':[30] the distribution of responsibility across the design of these systems remains challenging because of the

---

[26] Morley and others, 'From What to How' (n 19).

[27] Hagendorff, 'Blind Spots in AI Ethics' (n 1).

[28] Andrew D Selbst and others, 'Fairness and Abstraction in Sociotechnical Systems', *Proceedings of the Conference on Fairness, Accountability, and Transparency* (ACM 2019) https://dl.acm.org/doi/10.1145/3287560.3287598 accessed 12 June 2022.

[29] Hagendorff, 'Blind Spots in AI Ethics' (n 1) 7.

[30] Helen Nissenbaum, 'Accountability in a Computerized Society' (1996) 2 *Science and Engineering Ethics* 25; A Feder Cooper and others, 'Accountability in an Algorithmic Society: Relationality, Responsibility, and Robustness in Machine Learning' (2022) http://arxiv.org/abs/2202.05338 accessed 7 June 2022.

number of hands that a project passes through from its initiation to its deployment.[31] An ML system is the result of various teams working together: from project formulation to data collection to model training and deployment and maintenance; in the process of teams handling separate stages of the project and passing them on, researchers, designers, scientists, project managers and a selection of other stakeholders interact and contribute to the eventual ML model. These stakeholders, in turn, have differing priorities and expectations around 'ethical AI'. As Schiff et al. have argued:

> engineers and computer scientists may see their responsibility as focused on the quality and safety of a particular product rather than on larger scale social issues, and may be unaware of the wider set of implications. Business managers and companies may see their responsibility as fiduciary, in producing high-quality products and revenue. This potentially creates *holes in responsibility* for addressing key well-being impacts of AI (emphasis added).[32]

These different expectations are also influenced by individual *cultures of production*: as Widder et al. have recently pointed out, it is one thing to try to inject accountability into models built by a single private company; it is another beast entirely when dealing with notions of 'Freedom 0' (the norm of freedom of use and build on code) that mark the culture of open source software communities.[33]

With the current gaps in regulation regimes, it appears that the designated actor expected to operationalize ethics has fallen on to AI practitioners themselves.[34] Indeed, this was the conclusion that Wong et al. came to in their analysis of existing AI Ethics toolkits: the 'work of ethics' the authors conclude, 'is often imagined to be done by individual data scientists or ML teams'.[35] Nonetheless, it is not immediately evident that such expectations are practical or fair. Expectations for practitioners to take the lead often places them in difficult positions – trading-off resources like the time and effort

---

[31]   Mark Findlay and Josephine Seah, 'An Ecosystem Approach to Ethical AI and Data Use: Experimental Reflections', *2020 IEEE / ITU International Conference on Artificial Intelligence for Good (AI4G)* (2020).

[32]   Daniel Schiff and others, 'Principles to Practices for Responsible AI: Closing the Gap' [2020] arXiv:2006.04707 [cs] http://arxiv.org/abs/2006.04707 accessed 14 March 2022.

[33]   David Gray Widder and others, 'Limits and Possibilities for "Ethical AI" in Open Source: A Study of Deepfakes' 12.

[34]   Jessica Morley and others, 'Ethics as a Service: A Pragmatic Operationalisation of AI Ethics' (2021) 31 *Minds and Machines* 239.

[35]   Richmond Y Wong, Michael A Madaio and Nick Merrill, 'Seeing Like a Toolkit: How Toolkits Envision the Work of AI Ethics' http://arxiv.org/abs/2202.08792 accessed 7 June 2022.

invested in speaking out about ethical conundrums against the need to work within expected project timelines.

Thus, this reliance on *practitioners making ethical decisions* rests on a number of key assumptions: first, that they understand the social and ethical implications of their work; and second, that they have the know-how and capability to make decisions to address these implications.[36] In practice, both assumptions have been impugned. As discussed above, practitioners often need the aid of key domain experts to understand the social consequences of their work. More importantly, expectations for practitioners to take the lead in building ethically aligned systems misses out the organizational contexts whose incentive systems may be ill-aligned with ethical work. Interviews conducted with practitioners have highlighted this point saliently: Orr and Davis found that AI practitioners, embedded within their organizations and a wider set of regulations, often distributed responsibility across a range of actors and attributed a modicum of responsibility to themselves.[37] Changing legislation – especially concerning data protection – would set the context for their decisions around model development. Nonetheless, the rapidly shifting nature of ongoing regulation regimes – recalling here the uncertainty that marks a frontier – offers a degree of flexible discretion for actors' choices. Organizational norms such as codes of conduct may in essence provide a guiding hand for practitioners' understandings of ethical responsibility. The result, as Orr and Davis write, is that:

> [their] participants felt bound by the expectations, mandates, interests, and goals of more powerful bodies. At the same time, practitioners have technical knowledge which those who commission (and often oversee) their work do not. Thus practitioners *cannot* act with full discretion, and yet *must* exhibit independent efficacy... Rather than singular attributions, practitioners evoked and moved between, a web of responsible parties.[38]

In other words, as Nissenbaum and others have previously argued, the accountability of ML systems remains a *relational* practice:[39] while practitioners possess a certain level of individual know-how and discretion regarding operationalizing ethics, their actions are very much guided by expectations of the organizations in which they are embedded in. Recent research into work practices within technology companies has revealed organizational blockages that practitioners face. As Rakova et al. note, 'practitioners have to

---

[36] Morley and others, 'Operationalising AI Ethics' (n 15).
[37] Will Orr and Jenny L Davis, 'Attributions of Ethical Responsibility by Artificial Intelligence Practitioners' (2020) 23 *Information, Communication & Society* 719.
[38] Ibid., 725.
[39] Nissenbaum (n 30).

navigate the interplay between their organisational structures and algorithmic responsibility efforts with relatively little guidance'.[40] In doing this, they have to 'grapple with lack of accountability, ill-informed performance trade-offs and the misalignment of incentives within decision-making structures that are only reactive to external pressure'.[41] What remains little discussed are incentive structures within organizations, such as business goals (working within budgets, for profit, etc) cannot be separated from the processes of ML production. Instead, as scholars working with data scientists have shown, it has been the case that technical and business goals are intertwined in corporate data science and AI/ML services.[42] In particular, Madaio et al.'s work with practitioners revealed how business pressures to ship products 'on time' disincentivized practitioners from working on normative and ethical concerns such as fairness.[43] These pressures not only structure the time that practitioners have to 'give' to ethics consideration, they also influence key performance metrics that are used to assess the fairness of AI systems. In more recent analysis, for example, Madaio et al. found that business imperatives led to the prioritization of certain stakeholders over others (e.g., customers over marginalized groups).[44]

Institutional Capture?

What exactly are the priorities of AI Ethics? Who decides these? Who offers solutions? What solutions end up being legitimized? As Jasanoff and Hurlburt previously argued in the context of gene editing, conceptualizing the responsible development and use of technologies requires constant awareness of 'who sits at the table, what questions and concerns are side-lined and what power asymmetries are shaping the terms of the debate'.[45]

---

[40] Bogdana Rakova and others, 'Where Responsible AI Meets Reality: Practitioner Perspectives on Enablers for Shifting Organizational Practices' (2021) 5 *Proceedings of the ACM on Human-Computer Interaction* 7:1, 2.

[41] Rakova and others (n 40).

[42] Samir Passi and Phoebe Sengers, 'Making Data Science Systems Work' (2020) 7 *Big Data & Society* 2053951720939605.

[43] Michael A Madaio and others, 'Co-Designing Checklists to Understand Organizational Challenges and Opportunities around Fairness in AI', *Proceedings of the 2020 CHI Conference on Human Factors in Computing Systems* (ACM 2020) https://dl.acm.org/doi/10.1145/3313831.3376445 accessed 13 June 2022.

[44] Michael Madaio and others, 'Assessing the Fairness of AI Systems: AI Practitioners' Processes, Challenges, and Needs for Support' (2022) 6 *Proceedings of the ACM on Human-Computer Interaction* 1.

[45] Sheila Jasanoff and J Benjamin Hurlbut, 'A Global Observatory for Gene Editing' (2018) 555 *Nature* 435.

While these questions may be broad, addressing them is fundamental for understanding how ethics come to be (or not) in practice. In the context of AI Ethics, the answers to this question are far from inconsequential. Much criticism has previously been raised about the types of views represented in AI Ethics documents and guidelines: Hagendorff, for example, has pointed to these documents being predominantly male authored. This, he continues, may have led to the prioritization of principles like accountability, privacy, and fairness over others like care, social responsibility, empathy, and welfare.[46] Others have also noted that initiatives specifically oriented towards ideas of the 'common good', or appealing towards a wider humanity, have often failed to include the participation of groups that stand to be most affected by the development and use of largescale AI systems.[47] Jobin et al.'s review suggests that countries in the Global South continue to be vastly underrepresented in the shaping of the field: this 'raises concerns about neglecting local knowledge, cultural pluralism and the demands of global fairness'.[48] Global power imbalances, complicated by dramatic differences in the availability of funding between public and private bodies, have deep implications for both AI research and the trajectory of AI Ethics.[49]

On the one hand, the underrepresentation of key groups in society, particularly marginalized communities, has meant that the field is predominantly shaped by a narrow band of stakeholders often with an overtly technocratic approach towards framing 'AI Ethics' and its purported solutions.[50] On the other hand, differently situated groups also tend to prioritize alternative consequences of AI. Research examining ethics documents has revealed how variously situated actors prioritize different outcomes of AI innovation. Public sector organizations place more emphasis on questions of unemployment and economic growth while non-governmental organizations engage more with a broader range of ethical questions and challenges than both public

---

[46]   Thilo Hagendorff, 'The Ethics of AI Ethics: An Evaluation of Guidelines' (2020) 30 *Minds and Machines* 99.

[47]   Jean-Christophe Bélisle-Pipon and others, 'Artificial Intelligence Ethics Has a Black Box Problem' (2022) *AI & Society* https://doi.org/10.1007/s00146-021-01380 -0 accessed 14 February 2022; Emily M Bender and others, 'On the Dangers of Stochastic Parrots: Can Language Models Be Too Big? &#x1f99c', *Proceedings of the 2021 ACM Conference on Fairness, Accountability, and Transparency* (Association for Computing Machinery 2021) https://doi.org/10.1145/3442188.3445922 accessed 21 February 2022.

[48]   Jobin, Ienca and Vayena (n 12) 396.

[49]   Joel Klinger, Juan Mateos-Garcia and Konstantinos Stathoulopoulos, 'A Narrowing of AI Research?' [2022] arXiv:2009.10385 [cs] http://arxiv.org/abs/ 2009.10385 accessed 14 March 2022.

[50]   Meredith Whittaker, 'The Steep Cost of Capture' (2021) 28 *Interactions* 50.

and private sector organizations.[51] These distinct interests shape different approaches to the question of AI Ethics:

> For example, public sector documents focus on economic growth at the national level, while private sector documents emphasize technically 'fixable' and customer-focused issues, and NGO documents emphasize private sector accountability and a broader range of ethical issues.

All of this is a stark reminder that even in a field the responsibility for which has been to point out the fallacy of thinking about AI and ML as value-neutral or objective is 'not immune to the forces of politics and power'.[52] Politics and power in AI remain evolving forces to be unpacked and more thoroughly and critically examined. As Whittaker has written, the dominance of corporate resources in modern AI has meant that:

> the tech industry's dominance in AI research and knowledge production puts critical researchers and advocates within, and beyond, academia in a treacherous position. This threatens to deprive frontline communities, policymakers, and the public of vital knowledge about the costs and consequences of AI and the industry responsible for it—right at the time that this work is most needed.[53]

Given these critiques and concerns, moves have been made recently in both commentary and policy thinking to actively expand the diversity of voices at the table for decision-making. Participatory mechanisms, for example, have been built as a counterweight to the interests and influence of private actors in hopes that they can 'mitigate the risk that AI processes will be "captured" by actors who do not pursue the public good'.[54] Yet, even here, existing work suggests that much work remains to be done. In their research on AI Ethics guidelines, for example, Bélisle-Pipon and his colleagues hypothesized that these guidelines, which often included calls for participatory mechanisms to be included in the design and deployment of AI, would involve more stakeholders into their crafting. Yet the results of their analysis showed that not only did most organizations not include *how* they came to their normative conclusions; less than half their dataset of 47 documents indicated the involvement of external stakeholders in their development.[55]

---

[51]   Daniel Schiff and others, 'AI Ethics in the Public, Private, and NGO Sectors: A Review of a Global Document Collection' (2021) 2 *IEEE Transactions on Technology and Society* 31.

[52]   Hickok (n 17) 41–42.

[53]   Whittaker (n 50).

[54]   Christopher Wilson, 'Public Engagement and AI: A Values Analysis of National Strategies' (2021) *Government Information Quarterly* 101652.

[55]   Bélisle-Pipon and others (n 47).

Current efforts at expanding stakeholder engagement are also plagued by operational issues: such as what makes participation meaningful? At what point in the development process should stakeholders be consulted? What forms of participatory initiatives are transformative rather than performative? These questions cannot only be levelled at product design, but expectations of participation are also changing governance intentions in the creation of standards that will come to guide AI development more generally.[56] The challenge here is to cultivate ways of meaningful participation that do not merely become forms of 'participant washing'.[57] As Mona Sloane and her colleagues have pointed out, the research domain is currently at a point where it is trying to incorporate more stakeholders meaningfully. What the authors highlight, in addition, is the necessity of a *cultural shift* in data science that we are similarly beginning to see being emphasized by other scholars – embodied most succinctly, perhaps, in the outcome-oriented Design Justice method developed by Costanza-Chock[58] – recognizing that participatory efforts must be long-term and continuous.[59]

Frictions in the Pipeline

The scope and depth of these challenges call for much more sustained research into the realistic potential of ethics as a force in AI governance. Discussions of ethical questions routinely accompany emerging technologies. With AI and ML, these questions seem to reappear in the media with an increasing frequency.[60] Each time headline grabbing incidents occur, they provoke a similar set of questions: would an ethics board have approved this? Are commitments to 'ethical AI' merely performative? How do we progress beyond 'ethics washing'?[61]

---

[56] Michael Veale and Frederik Zuiderveen Borgesius, 'Demystifying the Draft EU Artificial Intelligence Act' [2021] arXiv:2107.03721 [cs] http://arxiv.org/abs/2107.03721 accessed 3 March 2022.

[57] Schiff and others (n 51) 36; Mona Sloane and others, 'Participation Is Not a Design Fix for Machine Learning' [2020] arXiv:2007.02423 [cs] http://arxiv.org/abs/2007.02423 accessed 28 January 2022.

[58] Sasha Costanza-Chock, *Design Justice: Community-Led Practices to Build the Worlds We Need* (The MIT Press 2020) https://library.oapen.org/handle/20.500.12657/43542 accessed 21 February 2022.

[59] Sloane and others (n 57).

[60] See David Dao's 'Awful AI' collection for an updated list of what its compilers have called "more and more concerning the uses of AI technology are appearing in the wild", https://github.com/daviddao/awful-ai accessed 22 April 2023.

[61] Luciano Floridi, *The Logic of Information: A Theory of Philosophy as Conceptual Design* (Oxford University Press 2019).

What the previous section has pointed to is that the realm of 'AI Ethics' is riddled with questions of power. Discussions of capture and the uneven allocation of resources within the field of AI are particularly important because they cast doubt on how much change we can reasonably expect practitioners to make to their work because of ethical consideration, and whether, practitioners should become the arbiters of socially consequential ML systems to begin with. As the discussions show, these individuals have some room for manoeuvre in the production ecosystem even with ethical compliance, but both organizational power dynamics[62] and institutional cultures[63] are more likely to shape and incentivize their actions.

The way forward for genuine practitioner engagement in the realization of AI ethics, I suggest, requires a reframing of expectations. Rather than a mechanism designed to resolve principled challenges – for example, providing a fix for discriminatory datasets through the collection of more data, or a remedy for privacy through federated learning – ethics is most useful when it provides friction in the process of AI development and design. Its operational utility as a self-regulatory reality, as such, continues interestingly to be in its conceptual slipperiness and indeterminacy. This flexibility of interpretation and application encourages what Morley et al. have called a 'pragmatic version of Habermas's discourse ethics':[64] where discussions of principles and their practice continue to form a part of a 'rationalisation process that involves a fair consideration of the practical, the good and the just, and normally relies heavily on language (discussion), for both the emergence of agreed upon norms or standards, and their reproduction'.[65] Discussion, conversation, *talk* – the mechanisms that others have argued are key for organizational accountability[66] – are processes of discursive friction: talking about and through ethics requires elements of reflection, justification, and re-ordering motivations. Space for friction in the production pipeline potentially provides opportunities for discursively questioning and challenging the status quo, or, as Rességuier and Rodrigues have argued, 'a constantly renewed ability to see the new'.[67] Given the interdisciplinary work that goes into the production of AI and the many hands problem discussed above, the relevance of AI Ethics is in its encouragement of contestation; it is what Edwards and his colleagues have

---

[62]   Wong, Madaio and Merrill (n 35).

[63]   Widder and others (n 33).

[64]   Morley and others, 'From What to How' (n 19).

[65]   Ibid.

[66]   Ruthanne Huising and Susan S Silbey, 'Accountability Infrastructures: Pragmatic Compliance inside Organizations' (2021) 15 *Regulation & Governance* https://onlinelibrary.wiley.com/doi/10.1111/rego.12419 accessed 8 June 2022.

[67]   Rességuier and Rodrigues (n 16).

termed a form of 'science friction', referring to the 'difficulties encountered when two scientific disciplines working on related problems try to interoperate'.[68] Such friction, as Rességuier and Rodrigues remind us, is thus *generative* of new relations and new possibilities:

> Ethics in that sense is a powerful tool against cognitive and perceptive inertia that hinders our capacity to see what is different from before or in different contexts, cultures or situations and what, as a result, calls for a change in behaviour (regulation included). This is especially needed for AI, considering the profound changes and impacts it has, and is bringing to society, and to our very ways of being and acting. [...]
> Without a continuous process of questioning what is or may be obvious, of digging behind what seems to be settled, of keeping alive this interrogation, ethics is rendered ineffective. And thus, the settling of ethics into established norms and principles comes down to its termination.[69]

If we accept that AI Ethics is not essentially meant to provide solutions to ethical conundrums, this shifts the goalposts of what researchers, practitioners, and perhaps the public, might expect from the ethic research activation, and its corresponding practices. The continued relevance of ethics is not in its reassurance that AI products are transparent, just, or fair. *Instead, it is in the practical creation of friction points in the AI/ML ecosystem.* Rather than to 'move fast and break things', AI Ethics throws up checkpoints and slows down the momentum of AI development to ask critical questions and to unpack power relations in the production of AI systems. As Hagendorff has similarly argued, 'it is wrong to assume that the goal is ethical AI... AI Ethics must dare to ask the question where in an ethical society one should use AI and its inherent principle of predictive modelling and classification at all'.[70]

This reorientation may seem minor yet putting it into practice is difficult. There is an unquestioned inclination from organizations to reduce points of friction in production lines rather than to intentionally add them, with the awareness of the resources – time, money, expertise – that such measures will impact. Still, this reorientation may prove crucial if the disruptive regulatory relevance of ethics is to be realized. The discussion above has highlighted much larger, structural issues of power imbalances that mark current AI research and development: from funding to hardware and software accessibility, to setting the terms of debates around how AI ought to be used in public

---

68 Paul N Edwards and others, 'Science Friction: Data, Metadata, and Collaboration' (2011) 41 *Social Studies of Science* 667.
69 Rességuier and Rodrigues (n 16).
70 Hagendorff, 'Blind Spots in AI Ethics' (n 1).

systems.[71] Deep structural changes need to be made in organizational culture and communication pathways that go beyond the scope of this chapter. The discussion above, nonetheless, has also suggested that scholars working within AI Ethics have been challenging the boundaries of the field by calling out these power imbalances and bringing underdeveloped issues to light. This exposé includes bringing attention to the flipside of what happens in the oft-cited operational spaces of big tech firms like Google, Facebook, and Amazon and focusing on the '"margins" of technology development: the hidden, low-status, low wage labour at clickwork or labelling factories';[72] the social and environmental costs and impacts of training data and energy intensive AI models;[73] and a more introspective push towards interrogating revenue models and incentive mechanisms that work to steer AI research and innovation towards profit over justice or sustainability.[74]

The reorientation proposed here thus joins other calls for a cultural change in the development of AI. Such a change involves and requires more careful, critical transition and deliberation pathways to be embedded within the AI research, development, and innovation spheres. In practice, it means adjusting practices and outlooks up and down the production pipeline. Morley et al. have, for instance, argued that AI practitioners need to develop 'an understanding of the ethical implications of the products that they design by combining ethics theories… in mandatory courses…'. Further researchers working on AI Ethics ought to ensure that AI Ethics remain relatable to both practitioners and members of the public; and that policy makers and legislators would do well to reject the all-or-nothing logic of the Collingridge dilemma and accept that movements towards regulation can be made without compromising innovation.[75] Elsewhere, Hutchinson et al. have also pointed to the need for more research on the cultures of AI Dataset development that could reveal how:

> the deeply collaborative nature of much dataset work conflicts with 'disincentives to collect data that come from a system that emphasizes individual academic

---

[71]   Jobin, Ienca and Vayena (n 12); Mostafa Dehghani and others, 'The Benchmark Lottery' [2021] arXiv:2107.07002 [cs] http://arxiv.org/abs/2107.07002 accessed 13 March 2022; Dehghani and others; Klinger, Mateos-Garcia and Stathoulopoulos (n 49).

[72]   Hagendorff, 'Blind Spots in AI Ethics' (n 1) 8; Kira JM Matus and Michael Veale, 'Certification Systems for Machine Learning: Lessons from Sustainability' (2022) 16 *Regulation & Governance* 177.

[73]   Bender and others (n 47); Josh Cowls and others, 'The AI Gambit: Leveraging Artificial Intelligence to Combat Climate Change—Opportunities, Challenges, and Recommendations' (2021) *AI & Society* https://doi.org/10.1007/s00146-021-01294-x accessed 21 February 2022.

[74]   Klinger, Mateos-Garcia and Stathoulopoulos (n 49).

[75]   Morley and others, 'Operationalising AI Ethics' (n 15).

output'…, as well as relationships with other common ML myopias—especially common to the 'hacker culture' of ML…—that celebrate Alpha leadership, competition, and other masculine tropes.[76]

Paullada et al. have addressed this in their research on the production of datasets, arguing for the need for a 'turn in the culture towards more careful practices of development, maintenance, and distribution of datasets that are attentive to limitations and societal impact while respecting the intellectual property and privacy rights of data creators and data subjects'.[77] These interventions align well with the goal of creating friction points for the critical interrogation of the ways in which technology is created and used in and through society. The question remains, nonetheless, that deliberative points of friction nonetheless need to be practicable to change existing cultures of AI production. It is this challenge to which the last section of this chapter now turns.

THE ORGANIZATIONAL TURN IN AI ETHICS

Without disregarding or minimizing the importance of ongoing efforts dedicated towards developing initiatives to increase stakeholder – and in particular public participation – engagement in the creation of AI (as discussed earlier, and in other chapters of this book), this section suggests that given the challenges that the field faces in operationalizing AI Ethics, this enterprise can be aided by a research agenda that focuses more thoroughly on business cultures and organizational norms in the AI/ML ecosystem. Taking seriously the contrary influences discussed above *and* previous observations that 'social scientists, by taking their own calls to "open up" too literally, have been too quick to advocate public dialogue rather than focusing on faulty governance approaches that could have otherwise been their target',[78] this section asks: to what extent are current processes endeavouring to create points of generative friction, successful? Given that the bulk of initiatives have been aimed at ethical design, how do we encourage a reorientation that supports ethics as a form of *disruptive imagining?*

---

[76] Ben Hutchinson and others, 'Towards Accountability for Machine Learning Datasets: Practices from Software Engineering and Infrastructure' [2021] arXiv:2010.13561 [cs] 569 http://arxiv.org/abs/2010.13561 accessed 25 December 2021.

[77] Amandalynne Paullada and others, 'Data and Its (Dis)Contents: A Survey of Dataset Development and Use in Machine Learning Research' (2021) 2 *Patterns* 100336.

[78] Ulrike Felt and others, *The Handbook of Science and Technology Studies* (4h edn, MIT Press 2017).

Current initiatives aimed at encouraging ethical deliberation have placed a large commitment on the individual AI practitioner. As mentioned earlier, research suggests, however, that practitioners are often insufficiently equipped to face ethical challenges in the AI production pipeline. In their work looking into tools and practices that industry professionals use to implement ethics, for example, Vakkuri et al. highlighted that practitioners, despite being aware of ethical conundrums, often lacked support from their own companies for *how* to incorporate tools into their workflows.[79] In a similar vein, as Morley et al. have pointed out, their own research on the operationalization of AI Ethics has often rested on the assumption that *all* practitioners are 'aware of the ethical implications of AI, understand their importance, and are actively seeking to respond to them... but the problem is... we lack information about barriers and enablers, therefore we cannot know the best way to encourage widespread adoption of pro-ethical AI practices'.[80] Indeed, existing study suggests that not only do practitioners have a somewhat patchy understanding of AI Ethics; they are often more cognizant of compliance with existing data protection regulation.[81] Such a risk-based approach, as argued earlier, relegates AI Ethics back to being a 'fix' for ethical problems rather than a space for open deliberation. In other words, ethics merely becomes a process in the prevention of harm rather than an active and open-ended questioning of whether projects *should be* embarked on in the first place. Yet, as others have pointed out before, AI products can be legally compliant and still be unethical.[82]

One approach to address the patchiness of practitioners' understandings of ethical conundrums has been the call for educational programs for practitioners, data scientists, and computer engineers; and, in particular, to ensure the inculcation of virtue ethics.[83] Yet the problem with this response is that it risks over relying on practitioners to make good decisions. This thinking misses the forest for the trees. As discussed above, practitioners – regardless of their individual interest or commitment to addressing the social implications

---

[79] Ville Vakkuri and others, 'Ethically Aligned Design of Autonomous Systems: Industry Viewpoint and an Empirical Study' [2019] arXiv:1906.07946 [cs] http://arxiv .org/abs/1906.07946 accessed 15 March 2022.

[80] Morley and others, 'Operationalising AI Ethics' (n 15).

[81] Ibid.; Findlay and Seah (n 31).

[82] Morley and others, 'Ethics as a Service' (n 34).

[83] Kirsty Kitto and Simon Knight, 'Practical Ethics for Building Learning Analytics' (2019) 50 *British Journal of Educational Technology* 2855; Thilo Hagendorff, 'AI Virtues – The Missing Link in Putting AI Ethics into Practice' [2021] arXiv:2011.12750 [cs] http://arxiv.org/abs/2011.12750 accessed 11 March 2022; Judy Goldsmith and Emanuelle Burton, 'Why Teaching Ethics to AI Practitioners Is Important', *Thirty-First AAAI Conference on Artificial Intelligence* (2017) https://www.aaai.org/ocs/index.php/ AAAI/AAAI17/paper/view/14271 accessed 11 March 2022.

of their work – are not operating in a vacuum. Instead, there are historical, cultural, organizational and institutional conditions within the AI ecosystem that collectively work to structure and incentivize the practitioners' capacities for ethical engagement. As Rakova et al. note, 'whether designing, appropriating, modifying, or even resisting technology, human agents are influenced by the properties of their organisational context... Individuals must adapt to the organisational context and follow what is seen as successful and effective behaviour *within that setting*'[84] (emphasis added). Indeed, in interviews with practitioners, Morley et al. noted how practitioners would emphasize the challenges of 'justifying the additional time and resource costs associated with "pro-ethical" design, especially when there is no clear return on investment'.[85] Similarly, Rakova et al. argued that '[t]he impact of ML systems on people cannot be changed without considering the people who build them and the organisational structure and culture of the human systems within which they operate'.[86]

Focusing on education efforts and the role of the practitioner also unhelpfully diminishes the amount of work and effort that practitioners must put in to engaging with more responsible AI development practices. As Rakova et al. found through their interviews with practitioners, such work is often voluntary and not compensated, 'The volunteers for these investigations [of bias issues within models] went far beyond their existing role descriptions, sometimes risking their own career progression, to take on additional uncompensated labour to prevent negative outcomes for the company.'[87]

These observations thus demand a pause to think about the practicality and feasibility of existing efforts to operationalize ethical AI practices. Beyond the difficulties that practitioners face understanding the social implications of their AI products, their own organizations may be similarly ill-equipped to cede time to the frictions of contestation. This misrecognition of business cultures, organizational norms, and incentive systems may thus explain the 'tension between academic and industry practice... where people answering calls to action with practical methods are sometimes met with explicit discomfort or disapproval from practitioners working within large corporate contexts'.[88] The current structural and process myopia within cultures of AI production can thus also be traced to where present interventions are aimed – much more work might be done at the organizational and institutional levels of the AI ecosystem

---

[84] Rakova and others (n 40).
[85] Morley and others, 'Ethics as a Service' (n 34).
[86] Rakova and others (n 40) 19.
[87] Ibid., 11.
[88] Ibid., 2.

rather than to continuously focus on empowering AI practitioners to make ethical decisions in the course of their work.[89]

Responsible Practices and Incentive Structures

These observations about the difficulties in realizing the regulatory impact of ethics thus prompt a re-engagement with ideas about the operationalization of practices that might aid the realization of generative frictions in the production of AI systems. I offer a case study here of documentation practices to tease out the implications of how to conceptualize both the shift in both our expectations of ethical AI *and* the focus on interventions at organizational levels.

Documentation initiatives have been an area of research that has gained much traction as a means of moving towards more ethical AI. Datasets are often perceived to be one of the key factors in AI and ML progression. Benchmark datasets in particular, such as ImageNet,[90] were foundational for recent developments in computer vision and image recognition.[91] ImageNet, in particular, brought about particular uproar when Trevor Paglen and Kate Crawford's *ImageNet Roulette* art project, which allowed individuals to upload pictures of themselves to be classified by ImageNet categories, revealed the dataset's deeply racist and misogynistic categories that had been embedded within it. These datasets have also been uncritically used in the training of machine learning models. Recent work on datasets have, nevertheless, called attention not only to the problems within datasets, but also the social implications of how such datasets have been curated and used. Ethical questions here might be raised at the stage of data curation, for example, touching on areas of consent. In their research, for example, Keyes et al. showed that benchmark datasets provided by the National Institute of Standards and Technology in the United States (NIST) had included data from vulnerable communities that had been taken without their consent.[92] In addition, unethical labour practices often undergird the formation of large datasets, in which the building of such datasets have often involved the outsourcing of labour (annotating, labelling,

---

[89] Miles Brundage and others, 'Toward Trustworthy AI Development: Mechanisms for Supporting Verifiable Claims' [2020] arXiv:2004.07213 [cs] http://arxiv.org/abs/2004.07213 accessed 10 March 2022.

[90] Emily Denton and others, 'On the Genealogy of Machine Learning Datasets: A Critical History of ImageNet' (2021) 8 *Big Data & Society* 20539517211035956.

[91] Paullada and others (n 77).

[92] Os Keyes, Nikki Stevens and Jacqueline Wernimont, 'The Government Is Using the Most Vulnerable People to Test Facial Recognition Software' [2019] *Slate* https://slate.com/technology/2019/03/facial-recognition-nist-verification-testing-data-sets-children-immigrants-consent.html accessed 15 March 2022.

sorting, etc.) to precariously positioned and low-paid 'micro-workers'.[93] Such research has thus made it significant for practitioners, researchers, policy workers, and regulators to understand not only the content of datasets but also the contexts of their creation. As it stands however 'prevailing data practices tend to abstract away the human labour, subjective judgements and biases, and contingent contexts involved in dataset production'.[94]

These observations have led to researchers and advocacy groups arguing that the production of AI ought to be followed through with better documentation efforts. Effective and interventionist documentation efforts, as the argument goes, would enhance the transparency of both datasets used for training models and models themselves. Very much like the discussion of responsible and ethical AI, documentation practices and their associated challenges are not at all unique to AI production. Indeed, initiatives like these have a history of enhancing the transparency and legibility of complex systems as seen in engineering, safety science, and library science.[95] Notable projects over the past handful of years include Datasheets for Datasets,[96] The Dataset Nutrition Label,[97] Model Cards for model reporting,[98] and Annotation and Benchmarking on Understanding and Transparency of Machine Learning Lifecycles (ABOUT ML).[99] While their specifics differ, the primary goal

---

[93]   Paola Tubaro and Antonio A Casilli, 'Portraits of Micro-Workers: The Real People behind AI in France', *2nd Crowdworking Symposium 2020* (Research program 'Digital Future', Universities of Paderborn and Bielefeld 2020) https://hal.archives-ouvertes.fr/hal-02960775 accessed 21 February 2022; Paola Tubaro and Antonio A Casilli, 'Micro-Work, Artificial Intelligence and the Automotive Industry' (2019) 46 *Journal of Industrial and Business Economics* 333.

[94]   Paullada and others (n 77).

[95]   Eun Seo Jo and Timnit Gebru, 'Lessons from Archives: Strategies for Collecting Sociocultural Data in Machine Learning', *Proceedings of the 2020 Conference on Fairness, Accountability, and Transparency* (Association for Computing Machinery 2020) https://doi.org/10.1145/3351095.3372829 accessed 10 March 2022; Edwards and others (n 68).

[96]   Timnit Gebru and others, 'Datasheets for Datasets' (2021) 64 *Communications of the ACM* 86.

[97]   Kasia S Chmielinski and others, 'The Dataset Nutrition Label (2nd Gen): Leveraging Context to Mitigate Harms in Artificial Intelligence' [2022] arXiv:2201.03954 [cs] http://arxiv.org/abs/2201.03954 accessed 11 March 2022.

[98]   Margaret Mitchell and others, 'Model Cards for Model Reporting', *Proceedings of the Conference on Fairness, Accountability, and Transparency* (Association for Computing Machinery 2019) https://doi.org/10.1145/3287560.3287596 accessed 12 March 2022.

[99]   Inioluwa Deborah Raji and Jingying Yang, 'ABOUT ML: Annotation and Benchmarking on Understanding and Transparency of Machine Learning Lifecycles' [2020] arXiv:1912.06166 [cs, stat] http://arxiv.org/abs/1912.06166 accessed 12 March 2022.

and value propositions of these documentation efforts are broadly similar: to encourage the creation of metadata – i.e., data about datasets and/or models – that enhance the transparency of choices and decisions made in the production of said dataset and/or model that have or may have bearings on the eventual AI product created.[100] Documentation initiatives thus function as key sites of generative friction as they work to introduce reflexivity into the production of AI: 'the primary objective', argue the creators of Datasheets for Datasets,[101] 'is to encourage careful reflection on the process of creating, distributing, and maintaining a dataset, including any underlying assumptions, potential risks or harms, and implications of use'.

These documents, in addition, would encourage the smoother flow of information within and *across* different organizations comprising an AI system production pipeline. Within the creation and construction of AI systems, the complexity of its various moving parts – from teams working on data collection, to model development and training, to deployment –presents a coordination test for keeping track of sites of decision-making and value-imbued choices: '[model production] involves cross-functional teams with different expertise, iteratively building, testing, refining, deploying and monitoring AI models... these roles drop in and out of the different points of the AI model development lifecycle'.[102] This coordination challenge is not just complicated by a variety of moving parts, it is also implicated in the maintenance of systems *over time*, as such 'improved documentation helps developers with all stages of the lifecycle... we expect that improved documentation will particularly aid dataset developers in the maintenance phase, due to both collective amnesia and employee turnover'.[103] Better and more deliberate documentation promises to illuminate into the black box of AI development, enabling stakeholders to be better equipped to understand the limitations of their datasets and/or models, and allows for different stakeholders' accessing the model's lifecycle to understand the provenance and deployment of AI products. It is not surprising, as such, that some have suggest documentation initiatives can also

---

[100] Iain Barclay and others, 'A Framework for Fostering Transparency in Shared Artificial Intelligence Models by Increasing Visibility of Contributions' (2021) 33 *Concurrency and Computation: Practice and Experience* e6129.

[101] Gebru and others (n 96).

[102] David Piorkowski, John Richards and Michael Hind, 'Evaluating a Methodology for Increasing AI Transparency: A Case Study' [2022] arXiv:2201.13224 [cs] http://arxiv.org/abs/2201.13224 accessed 11 March 2022.

[103] Hutchinson and others (n 75).

be seen as first steps towards forms of external evaluations and future audits of AI products.[104]

Documentation efforts provide a generative friction rather than a fix to problems of bias and discrimination. Firstly, rather than promising to *resolve* existing problems such as biased and unrepresentative datasets, documentation trails function to track key value-laden decisions made in the collection, curation, and training of datasets and models. Secondly, in prompting practitioners to question the limits and possible problems of their datasets and models, these initiatives also require a *pause* in the uncritical generation of AI products and stimulates practitioner reflexivity. Where are training datasets coming from? How have they been curated? What are the limitations of such datasets? Thirdly, documentation practices are also generative in that they function as informational devices for recognizing both the organizational complexity and the difficulties of maintaining AI products over the course of their use. As informational devices, systematic documentation also serves to expose the broader organizational contexts of AI production. Implemented successfully, they thus potentially offer a normative purpose as sites of friction in the forward momentum of AI production by providing detail about how principles may (or may not) be realized through process. They also have an instrumental function by creating a paperwork trail that both supports the maintenance of AI products and authorizes efforts towards auditing and verifying systems.[105] Documentation, as such, makes real and legible the human-machine hybridity that are AI systems.

Given the academic support for such initiatives,[106] how feasible are documentation efforts? Existing research continues to highlight key barriers reflecting the impediments discussed above. In the context of documentation efforts key questions remain: Who bears the responsibility for filling in and updating these documents? Will such work be voluntary? *Should* it be compensated? Research conducted in Singapore has, for example, highlighted how the time and effort needed to generate these documents remains a barrier to their adoption. Interviews with AI practitioners revealed how individuals were open to adopting better documentation practices but were also aware that comprehensive documentation efforts would compromise the amount of time they were able to spend on other aspects of their work.[107] Elsewhere, Piorkowski and his

---

[104] Shahar Avin and others, 'Filling Gaps in Trustworthy Development of AI' (2021) 374 *Science* 1327.

[105] Brundage and others (n 89).

[106] As of the time of writing, both Gebru et al.'s work on Datasheets for datasets and Mitchell et al.'s 'Model cards for model reporting' have both been cited more than 700 times.

[107] Findlay and Seah (n 31).

colleagues similarly conducted usability studies on *Factsheets*. Practitioners in their study reported substantial time commitments – with reporting times between six–24 hours – required for documentation. Similar feedback has also been collected from researchers who originally proposed such documentations: the Data Nutrition Project team, for example, noted that 'many data scientist want to do the "right thing" when it comes to address issues in data, but often *don't have the time* or expertise, or an available tool, to identify the relevant information' [108] (emphasis added).

It is notable that this trade-off between *time to do their 'actual jobs'* and what is seen to be an *optional* best practice has long been a question for software developers. As Edwards and his colleagues write:

> Just as with data themselves, creating, handling, and managing metadata products always exacts a cost in time, energy, and attention... Scientists typically experience this frictional cost as an additional burden on top of their primary work. Research scientists' main interest, after all, is in *using* data, not in describing them for the benefit of invisible, unknown future users, to whom they are not accountable and from whom they receive little if any benefit.[109]

The existence of such perceived trade-offs is a key area that ethical AI research needs to take seriously. Negotiating ethical applications is an operational reality and therefore documentation on the way to charting ethics realization will also need adjustment in different contexts. Now, it continues to appear that existing cultures of AI production work *against* the systematic, intentional documentation of datasets and models. Here, as discussed above, cultures of solutionism and hacker cultures work to 'devalue the incremental and cooperative care required to create high quality datasets'.[110] Indeed, as Rakova et al. have shown in their work looking into existing gaps in organizational practices, 'prevalent practices can place the burden of responsibility and labour squarely on individuals who identify issues and try to change outcomes within existing structures'. The lack of organizational norms available to incentivize individuals towards adopting better practices means that:

> [in] pushing for changes in [their organisation's] structures and processes... their goals... maybe antithetical to what is currently supported by the organisational structure. Thus, individuals who want to bring responsible AI issues into their work must do their own jobs, do the responsible AI work if that is not their official job, do the difficult work of redesigning organisational structures around them to accommodate the responsible AI work, and on top of it all, do the change management to

---

[108] Chmielinski and others (n 97).
[109] Edwards and others (n 67) 673.
[110] Hutchinson and others (n 75).

get those new organisational practices adapted. As a result, incentives may appear misaligned between individuals and their organisational context.[111]

Scholars working on documentation initiatives and other ethical AI practices have suggested that such changes need to occur. Indeed, rather than focus on 'explicit *normative* considerations' that individuals have to make such as educational programs for data scientists and engineers, Hutchinson et al. have argued that advancing a more critical technical practice might be achieved by directing efforts towards changing *organizational* structures, such as 'the need for properly budgeting for maintenance and treating it properly as 'repair work'... for redressing dataset technical debt, and for organisational recognition and rewards for data work'.[112] Similarly, Gebru et al. have acknowledged in their work that the 'the process of creating a datasheet will always take time, and organisational infrastructure and workflows – not to mention incentives – will need to be modified to accommodate this investment'.[113]

Presently, what remains less clear are the types of organizational changes and incentive structures that might effectively work to encourage the adoption of systematic documentation efforts. As such, amid a burgeoning literature of how to best put the goals of AI Ethics into practice, much more research ought to be done at the level of the organization to understand how and why certain practices – such as popularly supported ones like documentation efforts – are adopted, how they become adapted, and why they succeed or fail at incentivizing a change in the cultures of AI production. Or, to paraphrase Rakova et al, we need to understand why some organizations are differentially success at implementing practices of ethical AI.[114]

Here, then, we bring the analytical gaze away from placing the burden of responsibility for achieving ethical outcomes on the individual and focus instead on organizational and institutional contexts that structure current AI production. This change in focus also prompts a reformulation of what the field's practical research agendas may be: building on Schiff et al.'s observation that public, private, and non-governmental organizations often prioritize different aspects of ethical AI and Hickok's critique that ethical AI has rarely 'question[ed] the business culture, revenue models, or incentive mechanisms that continuously push these products into the markets',[115] similar lines of questions might be levelled at different organizations that sit within the AI production pipeline: how does funding decisions lead to the adoption (and

---

[111] Rakova and others (n 40) 18.
[112] Hutchinson and others (n 75).
[113] Gebru and others (n 96).
[114] Rakova and others (n 40).
[115] Hickok (n 17) 43.

justification) of certain practices over others? Do bigger technology firms have more leeway for the creation of ethics boards and ethical oversight compared to start-ups? If so, how do well-funded and well-resourced organizations 'set the agenda' for responsible AI as a result, and what practices might get locked-in when generalizing ethics attribution and distribution? Not only would these lines of questioning better respect the time and effort that AI practitioners have to devote to operationalizing ethical AI, but they also enable a more fine-grained analysis of the field and a more specific treatment of AI practitioners who continue to be regarded as a monolithic unit despite working within different industries, sectors, and companies with distinct business cultures and organizational norms.

Learning From Other Accountability Systems

The analysis in this chapter has drawn much from research on efforts to institute responsible practices within the ML production pipeline. It builds on existing calls for more organizational inquiries into how teams *across* the pipeline can communicate and take part in practices that promote transparency in the production of ML systems. For example, Deng et al. have argued for the necessity to 'explore how *teams* in organisations *collectively* use fairness toolkits on real-world tasks'.[116] This chapter agrees that a productive route for understanding current possibilities and challenges of existing toolkits lies in ethnographic studies conducted within organizations and suggests that these studies are also necessary for initiatives beyond achieving fairness. Such studies, in turn, must be complemented by interdisciplinary dialogues between designated researchers and policy makers working on AI governance and regulation.

Recent interest in licensing[117] and audits,[118] and the expansion of roles such as 'Chief AI Ethics Officer',[119] along with initiatives to improve ethics

---

[116] Wesley Hanwen Deng and others, 'Exploring How Machine Learning Practitioners (Try To) Use Fairness Toolkits' (2022) http://arxiv.org/abs/2205.06922 accessed 7 June 2022.

[117] Danish Contractor and others, 'Behavioral Use Licensing for Responsible AI' http://arxiv.org/abs/2011.03116 accessed 7 June 2022.

[118] Shea Brown, Jovana Davidovic and Ali Hasan, 'The Algorithm Audit: Scoring the Algorithms That Score Us' (2021) 8 *Big Data & Society* 2053951720983865; Sasha Costanza-Chock, Inioluwa Deborah Raji and Joy Buolamwini, 'Who Audits the Auditors? Recommendations from a Field Scan of the Algorithmic Auditing Ecosystem', *2022 ACM Conference on Fairness, Accountability, and Transparency* (ACM 2022) https://dl.acm.org/doi/10.1145/3531146.3533213 accessed 23 June 2022.

[119] 'Why You Should Hire a Chief AI Ethics Officer' (*World Economic Forum*) https://www.weforum.org/agenda/2021/09/artificial-intelligence-ethics-new-jobs/ accessed 15 June 2022.

education in computer science programs, professional certification, and the creation of standards is collectively shaping the professionalization of AI creation.[120] If so, there may be lessons that can be learned from other similar domains – health and safety, quality assurance, risk management, sustainability – that have a longer history within organizations that similarly had to reconfigure internal programs (trainings, procedures, communications, reporting structures) in accordance with external principled expectations. The combination of these programs – what Huising and Silbey have come to call 'accountability infrastructures'[121] – has faced similar challenges of allocating responsibility and aligning incentive structures. Existing research, the authors point out, 'shows that accountability systems and actors struggle to make their compliance mandates central to the organisation's strategic and operational routines'.[122] While perhaps painting a bleak picture for the future of AI Ethics, these existing infrastructures may nonetheless have much to offer for the study of organizational power dynamics that this chapter has explored.

CONCLUSION

This chapter has primarily concentrated on current efforts to realize ethical and responsible AI. In it, I have argued that for AI Ethics to maintain its relevance, we need to reframe its central challenges by shifting the locus of intervention (attribution and distribution of responsibility) away from the individual operative and on to the system of AI development itself. In addition, rather than seeing emerging practices such as AI audits as 'fixes' to thorny ethical conundrums, AI ethics must be recognized as a form of *generative friction* – a highly intentional and critical practice set in opposition to the forward momentum of technological progress.

At stake, I suggest, is a fragmentation of AI development that risks compounding existing structural inequalities across the Global North and South. Scholars and journalists have increasingly called attention to the inequities across AI developments in the Global North and South.[123] Not only are players

---

[120] Brent Mittelstadt, 'AI Ethics – Too Principled to Fail?' [2019] *SSRN Electronic Journal* https://www.ssrn.com/abstract=3391293 accessed 15 June 2022.

[121] Ruthanne Huising and Susan S Silbey, 'Accountability Infrastructures: Pragmatic Compliance inside Organizations' (2021) 15 *Regulation & Governance* https://onlinelibrary.wiley.com/doi/10.1111/rego.12419 accessed 8 June 2022.

[122] Ibid.

[123] Indermit Gill, 'Whoever Leads in Artificial Intelligence in 2030 Will Rule the World until 2100' (*Brookings*, 17 January 2020) https://www.brookings.edu/blog/future-development/2020/01/17/whoever-leads-in-artificial-intelligence-in-2030-will-rule-the-world-until-2100/ accessed 15 March 2022.

in the Global North dominating AI research and development, but they are also setting the terms of the debate on ethical AI—albeit with the exception of China. Some have started to call this a form of 'AI nationalism', or an emerging form of geopolitics between countries. Kai-Fu Lee has argued:

> [U]nless [developing countries] wish to plunge their people into poverty, they will be forced to negotiate with whichever country supplies most of their AI software – China or the United States – to essentially become that country's economy dependent, taking in welfare subsidies in exchange for letting the 'parent' nation's AI companies continue to profit from the dependent country's users.[124]

In the realm of ethical AI, others have similarly argued that 'AI governance guidelines risk being replicated across jurisdictions in a way that may be incompatible with the needs, goals, and constraints of developing countries, despite best efforts'.[125] Emerging regulation and national strategies can also be consequential for different national trajectories of how ethical AI plays out. In their discussion of key differences between the US's and EU's strategies of AI regulation, Roberts et al. point out the EU's prioritization of the protection of 'citizens' rights through outlining the guiding value of human-centric trustworthy AI, which anchors additional ethical principles',[126] while the US's primary considers economic competitiveness, leading to the adoption of a more self-regulatory governance approach. In the US context this has resulted in much ethics washing, shopping and anti-interventionist lobbying. In effect, the authors argue, 'the inadequacy of private sector regulatory measures has facilitated numerous harms, such as from biases in facial and emotion recognition techniques leading to discrimination'.[127] The absence of international regulatory mechanisms influencing and sometimes over-riding national regulatory self-interest is also posing risks in AI development through the phenomenon of ethics *dumping*: where the training and testing of questionable systems is increasingly being outsourced and exported to vulnerable populations in low- and middle-income countries.[128] As Roberts et al. highlight, 'criticism that the US has not adequately protected its technological and economic leadership,

---

[124] Kai-Fu Lee, 'Opinion | The Real Threat of Artificial Intelligence' *The New York Times* (24 June 2017) https://www.nytimes.com/2017/06/24/opinion/sunday/artificial -intelligence-economic-inequality.html accessed 15 March 2022.

[125] Shakir Mohamed, Marie-Therese Png and William Isaac, 'Decolonial AI: Decolonial Theory as Sociotechnical Foresight in Artificial Intelligence' (2020) 33 *Philosophy & Technology* 659.

[126] Huw Roberts and others, 'Achieving a "Good AI Society": Comparing the Aims and Progress of the EU and the US' (2021) 27 *Science and Engineering Ethics* 68, 68.

[127] Ibid.

[128] Mohamed, Png and Isaac (n 125).

nor prevented ethically concerning uses of its technologies for repression else-where... In fact, the US is one of the most prominent exporters of surveillance technology globally'.[129]

These are deep structural problems that will require disruptive regulatory efforts that go beyond the bridging of the gap between principles and practice towards international cooperation and coordination in AI governance. The question that remains for the regulatory future of AI Ethics is whether its efforts can in part speak to these deep structural problems. This chapter proposes that it can, and that the value of AI Ethics lies in its capacity to continuously challenge the status quo and reorient the collective gaze towards more just and socially beneficial uses of AI through upending the power arrangements that appear in its production pipeline. What does this mean in practice? For starters, stepping away from the idea that ethical action comes from a choice that indi-vidual practitioners make in the building of AI products, away from the idea that *responsibility* for harmful or discriminatory uses of AI lies in the hands of a single individual. Instead, the chapter's view of AI Ethics attribution and distribution recognizes that there are organizational (e.g., business cultures, variances in funding levels) and institutional (e.g., the presence and absence of laws, benchmarks, and auditing infrastructures) mechanisms that limit what control individual practitioners have in the ethics-contested decision-sites in their day-to-day jobs. Ongoing efforts to bridge the gap between ethical prin-ciples and practice, as such, must not place the burden and responsibility for change on the individual practitioner. Instead, as I have argued above, a more fruitful direction is to understand the decision-making context influenced by the current landscape of organizational incentive structures at the meso-level of AI production. While arguments like these are not novel,[130] current research focusing on the challenges that AI practitioners face – lack of standards, lack of sufficient industry buy-in for auditing mechanisms, lack of domain-specific knowledge[131] – suggest that both meso-level incentive structures, particularly

---

[129] Roberts and others (n 126).

[130] Miles Brundage and others, 'Toward Trustworthy AI Development: Mechanisms for Supporting Verifiable Claims' [2020] arXiv:2004.07213 [cs] http://arxiv.org/abs/2004.07213 accessed 10 March 2022; Shahar Avin and others, 'Filling Gaps in Trustworthy Development of AI' (2021) 374 *Science* 1327.

[131] Kenneth Holstein and others, 'Improving Fairness in Machine Learning Systems: What Do Industry Practitioners Need?', *Proceedings of the 2019 CHI Conference on Human Factors in Computing Systems* (ACM 2019) https://dl.acm.org/doi/10.1145/3290605.3300830 accessed 11 June 2022; Sasha Costanza-Chock, Inioluwa Deborah Raji and Joy Buolamwini, 'Who Audits the Auditors? Recommendations from a Field Scan of the Algorithmic Auditing Ecosystem', *2022 ACM Conference on Fairness, Accountability, and Transparency* (ACM 2022) https://dl.acm.org/doi/10.1145/3531146.3533213 accessed 23 June 2022.

those outside Europe and the US, are not well-understood and remain insufficiently addressed. By adopting and promoting generative frictions in the production pipeline – such as documentation efforts discussed above – and studying the operationalization of these frictions within organizations can prove to be valuable steppingstones towards deeper accountability infrastructures that are being freshly built to regulate the use and deployment of AI.

Given the scope of these gaps and the larger socioeconomic and geopolitical challenges that mark our current moment in global change – global warming, energy deprivation, food shortages – to purposefully advocate for another form of friction at such a time of crises may appear to be antithetical to a desire for orderly technological expansion: we want speedy solutions to pressing problems. Yet to reorient the gaze towards *systems* of AI production rather than the individuals who make up these systems means that a much larger buy-in across the AI production pipeline is obviously required if techno solutions are to occur in an atmosphere of responsible governance. Ideally, not only will technologies built under the banner of 'Tech for Social Good' be sustainable and address these crises for more than short-term economic gain and hollow moral legitimacy, but the accountability infrastructure that undergirds these technologies will be robust. Practitioners will be given the space as well as the ability to scrutinize their own work and effect ethical change; companies will open themselves up without loss to internal and external audits while engaging with a wider array of stakeholders; individual users and citizens who in turn will be capable of contributing to and interrogating responsible data use and models that they are impacted by. This chapter, and those preceding it, offer starting points for the imagination of a different world: one marked by a rejuvenated set of social and regulatory infrastructures that rest on and reflect on critical thinking about, these increasingly ubiquitous and often misunderstood ecosystems and their good governance.

5. Modelling disruptive regulation

The purpose of this concluding reflection is to draw some of the common themes from the case-studies presented in the body of the text when considering disruptive regulation, and to suggest how a regulatory model, respecting these themes might be crafted.

It is clear that the notion of 'disruption' argued for here, includes:

- Shifting a main motivation for regulation to power dispersal in favour of currently vulnerable stakeholders (be they trusting recipient communities, ill-informed data subjects, or overborn and alienated ecosystem players);
- Repositioning AI and big data from being the regulatory problem onto participating in the regulatory solution;
- Locating AI in both objects and outcomes of regulation to 'irritate' some of what we identify as the socially destabilizing features of disruptive economies; and
- Challenge some accepted qualifiers of frontier tech and data use (such as trust and ethics) to address the reasonable (and sustainable) expectations of vulnerable stakeholders in data markets, and front-line ecosystem players/ operatives.

It is one thing to assert the benefits of a new regulatory direction and another to give it form as a governance mode. Some practical applications of inclusive participatory regulation were posed in the first chapter. Trust as regulation is posited through relationships where recipients are fundamentally engaged in relating to AI in community, and requiring data usage that can found informed trust rather than create agnostic cultures of convenience. Additionally, organizational communication pathways throughout the AI ecosystem require regulation in favour of workers and consumers, and not only management and absentee shareholders. Digital self-determination necessitates that stakeholders in data relationships negotiate mutual interests in safe data spaces, to rehabilitate the market position of data subjects. Ethics as friction points in the transit of AI across the design ecosystem change the expectation for ethics from fixing a problem to exposing the internal and external forces at work against principled decision-making.

Within these different snapshots of disruptive regulation, we have proposed novel ways of envisaging and actioning otherwise more conventional regulatory components and outcomes – relational trust, communal autonomy, invasive ethics. New appreciations of participating in the regulatory project, particularly for those who up until now have at best received paternalist attention, should also allow for other core elements and applications of tech and data dynamics to positively contribute to governing the advance of new tech/data frontiers. Most obvious of these is the conscious shift away from the market benefit said to be offered by disruptive economies (utilising AI assisted information platforms and hijacking personal data), towards sustainable social relations between human communities, AI and data usage.

A succesful regulation regime will contribute to good governance strategies overall. In the case of frontier technology and mass data use these important contributors to the modern (and potentially positive players in managing global crises and ensuring global sustainability) have principally been directed to the profit purposes of exchange economies and commodity markets. For instance, instead of protecting indigenous knowledge and cultural heritage, blockchain has been reduced to a ledger servicing rapacious cryptocurrencies. As with blockchain and alternative currency frames, these have been lauded by proponents and profiteers as beyond external regulation, and not requiring legal measures of probity. Recent collapses in crypto exchanges have proved these asserions to be false.

This rejection of anything but internal and *light mode* self-regulation from the major info-tech platforms and digital finance networks, where ethics is talked but not mandated and compliance with organizational codes of good behaviour is argued for but not accountable, has set the tone for radical market disruption. It is small wonder that disruptive economies which these fascilities operationalize, have steadily undermined conventional employment and consumer servicing conventions in the name of authonomy, stakeholder choice, and rejection of old ways. Recently, courts across Europe and the UK have cast serious doubt on the wisdom, fairness and indeed legality of these incursions. With the proposed EU AI legislation, and the return to legislative controls on data use in China and other jurisdictions it seems that states at least are no longer willing to leave regulation in the realm of self interest.

This book is not arguing for some wholesale regression to previous market and social regulatory modes, although as with organized labour and gig work, this may not be such a bad idea. Instead, the twist from disruptive economies to their disruptive regulation employing AI and data as tools in this transition, not only has a potential to sharpen both internal and external regulation options but, it is argued, will fundamentally change a central motivation for valuing AI and mass data.

If there is a move to consciously motivate frontier technologies and mass data use towards communal/public benefit, and thereby make market/profit advantages more sustainable, our case needs to happen in regulation and governance policy. Any such materialization must be more than the project of state authority. COVID surveillance control policies saw many examples of collapsing public and private data. Smart cities advance in data use environments where traditional separation between public and private data is no longer mandated. This confluence is presenting particular challenges for *separation of powers* governance thinking. If public law is not designed to manage public administration, and private law to marshal private market arrangementswhere data use is concerned, then the need is pressing to involve public and private data use interests in data governance well beyond jurisdictional boundaries.

The proposition of a detailed regulatory strategy embodying disruptive principles and precesses as set out in this book requires more consideration than this brief concluding reflection allows. Indeed, once the nuts and bolts (and interoperability of these) are worked through there is the greater challeng to incorporate disruptive regulation into the larger debate about AI and mass data global governance. While hoping what has been so far here presented will provide a solid foundation for these developments, it would be remiss not to at least speculate on some practical directions for regulatory modelling in this vein.

In settling some more specific common features of the disruptive regulation case-studies provides, it is instructive to return to Black's definition and see how the 'disruptive' dimensions mentioned above translate into key regulatory components and how this is done.

> ... the sustained and focused attempt to alter the behaviour of others according to defined standards or purposes with the intention of producing a broadly identified outcome or outcomes, which may involve mechanisms of standard-setting, information gathering and behaviour modification.

Sustained – a disruptive regulation strategy needs to ground its commitment to fundamental power dispersal through applying AI and data for the informed enablement of currently-vulnerable stakeholders via information looping, and to maintain this empowerment by creating and sustaining opportunities for inclusion and engagement in the regulatory mission.

Focused – the regulatory strategy is critical, anticipating resistance to this sustained redirection of power through efforts to capture newly empowered stakeholders, rather than concede to mutualized interests. Capture can be exposed and thwarted by requiring internal and external accountability and transparency whenever relationships of AI dependency are formed.

Altering the behaviour of others – presently in the disruptive economy discourse conventional market arrangements of obligation and duty are being altered under the guise of stakeholder empowerment (through self-determination as a highly individualist exercise). Additionally and perhaps more

disruptive, these behavoural changes are creating new, insidious and disempowering data dependencies through platform market immersion. The
behavioural change envisaged via disruptive regulation foresees fundamental
reshaping of the relationship between humans and AI/data usage so that AI
facilitates community bonding and thereby generates trust by employing
ethical decision-making at key-points in the ecosystem and the deployment
chain.

Defined standards & purposes – it is here that disruptive regulation moves
away from neo-liberal market economics and their preference for ungoverned
self-regulation. While not rejecting a wealth creation purpose for the application of AI and big data, disruptive regulation does not see *wealth* only in
monetary terms, nor does it accept that the beneficiaries of such wealth should
be restricted to the creators, marketers and traders in technology and data. The
standards for this form or regulation are emancipated ethical principles that
generate genuine and sustainable trust relationships and irritate dependencies
that exist in atmosphere of ignorance and acquiescence. Beneficiaries live in
AI-enabled communities and the purpose of their regulation is to promote and
distribute social wealth.

Broadly identified outcomes – Who identifies? – recipient communities
and communities of data subjects. How broad? – broad enough to escape
the bounds of market advantage (recognizing that these may also be worthy
of a reenvisaged protection) and to move into appreciations of *standing* not
limited to contractual ties, or market enrichment. The determination of purpose
will be contextually specific in different communities, but always governed by
the aim of reducing data power asymmetries.

Mechanisms – Black identifies the key components of the regulatory mechanisms that we tag as disruptive. They must not only work from complementary
and radical standards but advocate for these. They must gather information to
benefit those who suffer from structural and processual information deficit.
They must *modify* the behavioural accesses of market behaviours in disruptive
economies formulating and feeding of power asymmetries.

Information gathering and behavioural change – a powerful way to end
this short engagement with modelling is to emphasize the importance of
information in achieving behavioural change for social good. As the participatory self-regulatory frame suggested in Chapter 1, for gig workers and
platform economies, information deficits disempowering vulnerable stakeholders enable the more powerful data harvests to change the behaviour of
personal data as a commodity and create massive commercial and operational
advantage. The dependencies for workers and customers, on the power of the
platform perpetuates relationships of blind obligation in which no real control
over the data produced by data subjects could be for them known, envisaged or
realized. Information deficit is at the heart of such dependencies and their dis-

empowering reach. AI-assisted information looping, as one tech solution, can de-fog such deficits and provide the understandings essential for data-subjects not only to approach the regulatory table but to have the knowledge necessary to negotiate data access and use to their benefit.

Perhaps the recurrent and pressing object for the regulation and governance of personal data use (and the AI technologies that facilitate it) is digital/data dependency. Some of these dependencies are very convenient, even uniquely advantageous for data subjects. However, when they are generated and maintained in an atmosphere of conscious data disempowerment perpetuated by data harvesters (featuring in many of the commercial contexts that comprise disruptive economies) then the behavioural change achieved as a result of regulation must disrupt the role of AI and data in the market, enabling AI and data to disrupt disempowering dependencies. Otherwise, not just the public benefit that can come from tech and data is at risk, but the medium-term sustainability of dependency-based economies will falter as data-subjects withdraw trust from the data access process.

Index